DETROIT'S
LOST POLETOWN

The Little Neighborhood that Touched a Nation

Brianne Turczynski

THE
History
PRESS

Published by The History Press
Charleston, SC
www.historypress.com

First published 2021

Manufactured in the United States

ISBN 9781467145794

Library of Congress Control Number: 2020945742

Notice: The information in this book is true and complete to the best of our knowledge. It is offered without guarantee on the part of the author or The History Press. The author and The History Press disclaim all liability in connection with the use of this book.

Dedicated to the memory of Jeanie Wylie-Kellermann,
author of Poletown: Community Betrayed,
and Father Joseph Karasiewicz, beloved priest of Immaculate Conception

CONTENTS

Author's Note   7
Preface   11
Acknowledgements   17
Introduction   21

THE LOST NEIGHBORHOOD: A HISTORY   27
  Poletown: What's in a Name?   27
  Safety in Numbers   30
  Polish Traditions Practiced in Poletown   33

NEIGHBORHOOD LANDMARKS   37
  Dodge Main   37
  St. Joseph's Hospital   39
  Beth Olem Cemetery   40
  Hervey C. Parke School   43
  John F. Majeski School   44
  Immaculate Conception   45

WHAT THE CHILDREN OF POLETOWN REMEMBER   51
  Candy Kitchen   51
  Home Theater and Iris Theater   53
  Potato Chip Central   54
  Roaming the Neighborhood   54
  "Everybody Knew Everybody"   56
  Choir Kids and Altar Boys at Immaculate Conception   60

CONTENTS

THE BEGINNING OF THE END   63

A Highway Runs Through It   63

The Riots of 1967   64

Holding onto the Roots of Polonia   66

What About the Churches?   68

St. John the Evangelist   71

Troubled Times at Immaculate Conception   73

THE POWERS-THAT-BE   77

Rumor or Truth?   77

General Motors and Coleman Young   80

Dollars and Cents   82

Eminent Domain in the Case of Poletown   87

Celebration for Hamtramck   89

EXODUS   94

The Resistance   97

Looters and Arson   100

The Last Moments of Poletown   104

Farewell, Father Joe   116

REMNANTS OF DETROIT'S LOST POLETOWN   118

On the Film *Poletown Lives!*   118

The Scholarly Book *Poletown: Community Betrayed*   119

The Bruce Harkness Photos   120

Pieces of Immaculate Conception   124

Epilogue   127

Notes   131

Index   141

About the Author   143

AUTHOR'S NOTE

Throughout this work, I have referenced the 465 acres of land in both Hamtramck and Detroit that were razed for the General Motors plant in 1981 as Poletown. I have put much emphasis on the Polish community in the neighborhood; the reader will notice little is mentioned of the many Black, Albanian, Yemenis, Armenian, Hispanic and Filipino residents of Poletown. The absence of their voice in the story is not done to discount them; however, story features about other ethnic groups were rare in the media. The focus was kept primarily on those who fought the plant and the progress of the plant itself.

Families like the Feagans, for example, who owned a lawn mower repair shop on I-94 and Mount Elliot, also fought the General Motors plant. Mr. Feagan enjoyed playing blues on his guitar and sometimes played at his church, Greater Triumph Baptist Church, in Poletown. In my research, I have read just about every article written at the time; the reporters seemed to keep a close eye on the efforts of both the Polish Neighborhood Council and Ralph Nader's organization, Center for the Study of Responsive Law, as well as the progress of the plant and the politicians and businessmen involved. But the reader should know that the neighborhood of Poletown was extremely diverse, *beautifully* diverse. Many residents commented that the neighborhood was rich in various cultures and beliefs and everyone got along. Forgotten tidbits were menial compared to the bigger story but are still worth mentioning here. There was Carl Fisher, a second-generation Grecian, who owned the Famous Bar-B-Q restaurant on Chene Street. He said his customers were black, white,

Poletown children posing for a picture on Easter Sunday, 1981. *Bruce Harkness.*

Italian, you name it, but everyone got along. He commented that during the 1967 Riot or the 1967 Rebellion, as it's sometimes called, these same diverse customers called him up and offered to watch over his restaurant at night. John Smigielski mentioned in an interview with me that the neighborhood kids who were every ethnicity other than Polish would always say hello to his elderly mother and ask her if she was all right, if she needed anything, as she swept her upstairs balcony at the family funeral home. Then there is the story about the Albanian congregation that took over the pews at Immaculate Conception in overwhelming numbers every Sunday at two o'clock in the afternoon, women on one side, men on the other. And let's not forget the sad anecdote that somewhere in a storage unit, or in a basement, or maybe even rotting in a dump are all of John Saber's personal reels from World War II and his own photographic collection of the demolition of his neighborhood, lost in the haste of his relocation.

The story of Poletown is centered on the drama that resulted from the illegal use of the eminent domain law and those who tried to save not only the doomed neighborhood but also the Immaculate Conception Catholic church. The church, the Immaculate Conception, became the center for the resistance and the symbol of the fight for justice. It still held Mass in Polish every Sunday in 1981. I felt that this was an American story that budded out of the roots of Polonia. As the reader will learn, the fight was something in the blood of those men and women, generations-old pride for the old country they had built in the new—free from communism. Their enthusiasm set off a ripple effect to other activists who heard about their gatherings at Immaculate Conception, when they formed the Polish Neighborhood Council fueled by the political angst of Tom Olechowski. Many thought it was comical that older women were protesting the General Motors plant, and some reporters used this fact to add a little comedy to their reports.

In this work, you will see that I used some of the same quotes Jeanie Wylie-Kellermann also highlighted in her book, *Poletown: Community Betrayed*. Some of this was coincidental, as I'm sure she and I used many of the same news articles. Other times, if I felt what she featured was vital to the story, then I included it here. Many documents concerning Poletown have since been donated to archival collections, meaning I had access to letters and evidence that Jeanie did not, so on some accounts the reader will see a touch more detail, but her book is extremely thorough.

Some reporters spewed vinegar at the Poletown residents who resisted relocation, while others were mostly indifferent. In my research and interviews, I have heard just about every side of the argument. Greg Kowalski, executive director of the Hamtramck Historical Museum, for example, was quoted various times in support of the GM plant. In a recent interview with me, Kowalski defended himself by explaining the plight of Hamtramck at the time and how the project would save the small city, which is included in this work, but he also said that he hated the way the City of Detroit went about it—he did not like how they took the homes from people. This addition to his thought on the matter will usually be omitted by journalists trying to argue the injustice of the plant. In all fairness, I felt his full side of the story should not be omitted from this work. He was never entirely apathetic, as some reporters have painted him. I added this thought here instead of in the book itself because this section allows me to share my personal insight. There are some folks who don't know the in-depth story, and I think those who merely shrug their shoulders and argue that the neighborhood was blighted anyway, or that most people were happy to leave, missed the point entirely.

Although some people may have been "done" with the neighborhood and were ready to move on, there were some who were *not* ready and wanted to live out their lives there. They had a *community* in Poletown, and it was there they wanted the freedom to live.

PREFACE

In February 2019, I went to an estate sale in an old neighborhood of Detroit called Indian Village. Though I have been known to collect my fair share of antiques, I wasn't planning on buying anything. The home where the estate sale took place was large and beautiful. I moved through the dusty old rooms never thinking that I was about to stumble upon an object that would change my life.

As I entered one of the back rooms, I saw a broken and dirty stained-glass window on a nearby table for sale. The center was marked with the words "God Buildeth His Holy Temple." Immediately, I wondered what became of the church it once lit. I knew the window would cost a lot to fix. I usually steer clear of antiques that will cost more to fix than they are probably worth, but for some reason I knew I couldn't leave that house without the window. The guy who sold it to me said it was from one of the churches torn down when they built the Poletown plant. I didn't know what he was talking about. I had never heard of Poletown before.

I took the window to Jeff Warmuth at Canterbury Stained Glass in Pontiac. For a time, he lived in Hamtramck and suggested I should try to find out from which church the window came. He told me a little about Poletown and how they knocked down a lot of churches and a whole neighborhood to build the General Motors Assembly plant. That piqued my curiosity. That night, I went home and did some searching. I didn't find anything about the window, but I was up past midnight reading articles, looking at pictures, watching videos, the whole time in awe over the injustice of it. I was determined the

The window the author purchased and restored from an unknown Poletown church. *Author's photo.*

next day to go to the library and borrow a book titled *Poletown: Community Betrayed.* I had seen pictures of the author holding her book, but I paid little attention to her name.

The next day, *The Record*, the Episcopal Diocesan newsletter for Michigan, came in the mail. I casually thumbed through it and came across an excerpt from a book called *Dying Well.* It was a random addition about the life of the former editor of *The Record* who had died in 2005. I was confused by the fact that it was included in a 2019 edition of the newsletter. It marked no anniversary and had no real meaning for an unfamiliar reader like myself, except perhaps that it offered some reflection about its timing and my own mortality. I put the article down a little teary-eyed that a woman so young had to die.

I then journeyed to the public library to rent the book about Poletown. When I read the author section in the back, I realized the author, Jeanie Wylie, was the very woman I had just read about moments before in *The Record* who died in 2005.

After that, every word I read about Poletown seemed to have the whisperings of destiny, fate or Providence hidden somewhere therein. For a person like me who loves allegory and symbolism, the fact that this amazing journey began with a window is significant. Windows help us see into a space or help us see the world outside our own comforts. If they are dirty, they can make the view grim; if they are clean, they can make the view clear—thus, the very action of *seeing* is muddled or cleared by the condition of the "glass," or our own point of view, and windows also brighten a dark space. I like to think what had become of Poletown was a dark space, a void in history where an evil force had conquered the land, abused it, set it ablaze, put it to mediocre use and then tossed it aside. And that window, filthy and broken after years of neglect, lay there as if waiting for me. I got the window restored and cleaned and hung it in the front window of my home for all to see. I wrote this book to help restore the Poletown story, bring it into the light once more under a new sky, a new point of view. Perhaps the world is ready now to understand what the people of the neighborhood went through, how they fought. Their unwavering protest should be an inspiration to us all.

In 1980, the 465-acre neighborhood of Detroit was a living, breathing community. There were over 1,400 homes, 144 businesses and more than a dozen churches, not to mention schools, a hospital and over 4,200 residents. There were bakeries and restaurants famed for their barbecue and kielbasa. There were generations-old businesses like Stella Barowski's general store, where children would go to buy candy and ice cream sandwiches. But all this would be destroyed within a year by a signature on paper. In the eyes of media viewers at home, the fight for Poletown, all the protests and legal action by the residents, seemed overblown. "Why can't they just move?" was the question on every dispassionate tongue. GM's presence in the media was perpetually advertised as a hero, coming to pull Detroit out of or lessen the blow of a nationwide recession (caused by the declining prosperity of the auto industry) by offering to build a plant in Detroit that would supply six thousand jobs. But the people of Poletown fought still, however muted their voices might have been.

In the fall of 1980, letters from the City of Detroit were mailed out to let the neighborhood residents know their fate, and the people began to rally. The Immaculate Conception Catholic Church became the epicenter for the resistance efforts and the last breath of this community whose death certificate was already signed and notarized. Father Joseph Karasiewicz of Immaculate Conception, whom in this work I have often called Father Joe, was cautious when speaking out against the plan, as the archdiocese had already sold the church to the city for $1.3 million. But when Ralph Nader and his team showed up, Father Joe became more vocal about what he felt was an injustice even though he was ordered by the archdiocese to keep quiet.

In the fight for Poletown, the neighborhood built lasting relationships with several community outsiders. Gene Stilp and Jeanie Wylie-Kellermann, for example, were both arrested because of their nonviolent activism against what they knew to be the unconstitutional taking of a neighborhood. Some of the residents, stay-at-home mothers and elderly women, were surprised at the ways in which they rose against the injustice, willingly protesting in the streets. Then there was Teofilo Lucero, a Native American who supported the residents because he and others felt what was happening in Poletown was like what had happened to the Indigenous communities in America. Father Joseph Karasiewicz also found his voice and his calling in the matter, fighting for his people and *their* church with everything he had. His parishioners would go on to organize the group Friends of Father Joe to make time to reunite with one another again after Poletown fell, nurturing their comradery, like veterans after a war.

Some in the archdiocese accused Father Joe of being brainwashed by Ralph Nader. Eventually, Father Joe became one of the top spokespeople of the neighborhood, speaking out against the archbishop himself. This would evidently cause him to be somewhat ostracized by the archdiocese, and it was speculated that his sense of alienation and disillusionment led to his heartbreak and eventual death five months after the Immaculate Conception fell.

If anything, the resistance efforts in Poletown were evidence of what a community can do when it sticks together, allowing fellowship to reign even in the face of death or injustice. Even when the powers were trying to split and scatter the neighborhood, the residents instead became more united than perhaps they had ever been. If anything, despite how angry and hurt these people were, their protests were an act of passionate love for their neighbor, for their family, for their church, for their childhood memories and for their traditions. Theirs was the fight, with mute voices in the face of the media, for what's *real* in life. Yet the "powers" weren't listening; they were even calling the neighborhood, its community, a myth. The Poletown residents fought for the things we all should fight for and what we have fought for; theirs was the honorable fight, a fight for their *lives*. There was nothing materialistic or capitalistic about it. If we look at what—as a conglomerate—GM, the City of Detroit, the UAW and the Catholic Archdiocese were trying to gain out of the deal compared to the people of Poletown, those bending to material gain are plainly exposed. *This* is how we discern between the truth and the lie. It is the same discernment that took place in the hearts and minds of those activists and residents who helped the neighborhood fight—even when they doubted their own power to do so.

Though I did not grow up in Hamtramck or within the city limits of Detroit, I have been introduced to the Polish culture through my husband and his family. This work is meant to memorialize those affected by the destruction of the Poletown neighborhood. With this piece, my goal was to release certain documents and ideas from the archives. I wanted to put these materials into the hands of regular readers, materials that otherwise would be filed away in the dark indefinitely. I consider this work an oral history, a collection of firsthand accounts and witnesses of a neighborhood and a time that will never be again. It is a story to be passed down generation to generation. And I have felt like its mother in many ways through my journey with it—protecting all that I can, capturing and collecting knowledge of its past so that the future will remember and know that it indeed existed. Poletown was no myth. It was very real, and I'm sure, for a moment it was very wonderful. This work is a love letter to the neighborhood—wiped from the map—whose later people fought with more vigor and energy than most people do (or will ever have to) their whole lives, just to save their community.

ACKNOWLEDGEMENTS

First, I want to thank John Rodrigue, the acquisitions editor of The History Press, who believed in this book from the beginning, and all the good people at The History Press who have seen this work through. When I first became interested in Poletown and the people affected by the razing of the neighborhood, I of course read Jeanie Wylie's book, *Poletown: Community Betrayed*. While I was touched by each story of the victims, I was affected most of all by Father Joseph Karasiewicz and his heroism involved in this story. He inspired me, and I wanted to get to know him more. Though he had passed away, I called Gene Stilp, who worked for Ralph Nader's team during the razing of the neighborhood. He was a good friend of Father Joe. He gave me the idea to do a reunion documentary or something that would memorialize the event.

At the time, the task of making a memorial of any kind seemed very overwhelming, not to mention the fact that I was a suburban novelist and poet. I never drove to Detroit by myself, not for the fear of Detroit but the fear of being in unfamiliar places alone. I hated driving, especially on the highway. And as far as meeting new people and asking them questions, I could do it and with joy, but I would much rather stay at home and not be bothered. I would have made an excellent hermit. But an otherworldly pull nagged me to step out of my comfort zone and investigate the story further. I couldn't help the persistent feeling that the people who died and suffered needed closure somehow. For months, I was haunted by this thought.

Jeanie's book was a helpful start, but I craved a closer look at the people and the neighborhood itself. Gene Stilp was great in that he allowed me to call and ask him questions whenever I got the notion. His encouragement in the beginning is a big part of why this book exists.

Also, Jeanie's husband, Bill Wylie-Kellermann, was kind enough to meet me and talk about his late wife's work in Poletown. He gave me several books to read, one titled *Dying Well*, which is a collection of little snippets of Jeanie's life and documents written by Bill in beautiful, heart-wrenching detail, about her last years, days, minutes, seconds. This glimpse into her inspiring life of activism and faith created a backbone in my reasoning as to why the Poletown story was so important for justice-seeking activists and why it is still relevant today. The thirst for this story and everything I could learn about Poletown was unending. I was determined to get this story out into the hands of readers once more, so it was necessary to toss all fear aside to complete the job I believed I was mysteriously called to do. I love driving on the highway now.

I would like to also thank my neighbor Nina Ignaczak, who, in many ways, ignited a flame in me for investigative journalism and encouraged me to get in touch with The History Press about Poletown. And, of course, I couldn't have done it without my family, who were all very patient with me during the research process while I traveled to visit archives and conduct interviews. My husband, my mother, my in-laws and my grandma were called, often at the last minute, to be with my kids after school because I was always running late coming back from the city.

I want to thank the Hamtramck Public Library and its director, Tamara Sochacka, who kept newspaper clippings available to me whenever I needed them. I give my thanks to Greg Kowalski, Executive Director of the Hamtramck Historical Museum, who agreed to speak with me and offered images and documents necessary for the story. Thank you as well to the archivists at the Catholic Archdiocese, Steve Wejroch and Eric Morgel, who shared their workspace with me and invited me to lunch on several occasions when I visited to peruse the collections.

I will never forget the talented Bruce Harkness, who met me for coffee and spoke to me about his experience photographing the doomed neighborhood. He also shared images of his early years and images of Poletown for this book. Also, I need to thank the Walter Reuther Historical Library and its kind staff, the Bentley Historical Museum in Ann Arbor, and the Detroit Public Library for housing the Burton Historical Collection for public use. Also I give my thanks to Jim Jaczkowski, who allowed me to borrow his entire Poletown collection for this work and shared his family photos, and to David Wronski, who gave me permission to use his blog posts and the beautiful painting his wife, Michele Fillion, did of Poletown's Candy Kitchen. My thanks also to Bruce Garwood, who corresponded back and forth with me about the neighborhood for weeks on end. I also want to thank everyone who allowed me to interview them or took time out for me and this project that I have not yet named, including John Richard, Paul Stern, Deb Choly, Darlene Zabrzenski, John Smigielski, Alan Ackerman, Larry Geromin, Bishop Thomas Gumbleton, George Corsetti, Roy Feldman and Taro Yamasaki, the latter of whom I did not interview for this work, but we discussed the project over coffee at his home; I thank him for his hospitality and our conversation that day. I would also like to thank Patricia Siergiej-Swarthout, who allowed me to include some of her private family photographs and her touching poem about Poletown, her childhood neighborhood, in this book.

I also can't forget to thank the beloved Father Joseph Karasiewicz, whose face I could not shake from my mind since I began researching the neighborhood. On a cold, windy day last spring, I drove down to Mount Olivet Cemetery to visit his grave. Although I received a map and his grave's location from the nice ladies in the office, it took me an hour to find it. I had nearly given up when I decided to cross my first path again, and there it was, sunken and grown over and barely visible in the grass. Poor Father Joe. I moved some of the earth away using the heel of my boots and snapped a few photos and promised myself to return to plant flowers, but when quarantine began because of the Covid-19 pandemic later that same week and continued into the late spring, I didn't return. So if you, dear reader, find yourself near the Mount Olivet Cemetery, stop in and say hello to my friend. Because whoever can sympathize with this story is a friend of Father Joe.

I hope eventually more can be done to memorialize this event, but for now this book, which gave me the journey of a lifetime, will have to do. I only hope I have done it justice.

INTRODUCTION

Often, we live in a town ignorant of its history. We might go our whole lives walking the streets, talking to neighbors, frequenting bars and restaurants, without knowing about the earth below and who has made footsteps in the dirt before us. It might be surprising to anyone venturing into Detroit's history to find that in the beginning it was a vast meadow, a prairie with vineyards of wild grapes. And its landscape formed a vast orchard of fruit-bearing trees. Among these fruits were pears and peaches so tender and sweet that the area became known for its fruit-infused brandy in those early years of settlement.

I have walked the streets of Detroit many times, and I still cannot imagine away the concrete sidewalks, the skyscrapers and the break wall that has since eliminated the river's natural bank. An account of early Detroit was given not only by Antoine de la Mothe Cadillac but also by Father Louis Hennepin, who accompanied Robert Cavelier, Sieur de La Salle, during his expedition down what is now known as the Detroit River. His account is the very first written record describing the bank: "The banks of the straight are vast meadows, and the prospect is terminated with some hills covered with vineyards, trees bearing good fruit, groves, and forests so well disposed that one would think nature alone could not have made, without the help of art, so charming a prospect. The country is stocked with stags, wild goats, and bears which are good for food, and not fierce as in other countries."[1]

Detroit Riverfront along Belle Isle around 1910. *Library of Congress.*

From the river, they encountered a shallow beach and a small incline placing them on the spot that would be the city we know today. They called it *le Détroit* or the straits. When Cadillac saw it, he wrote a similar report back to Quebec:

> *The banks of the river are so many vast meadows where the freshness of these beautiful streams keeps the grass always green. These same meadows are fringed with long and broad avenues of fruit trees which have never felt the careful hand of the watchful gardener; and fruit trees, young and old, droop under the weight and multitude of their fruit, and bend their branches toward the fertile soil which has produced them....On both sides of this strait lie fine open plains where the deer roam in graceful herds, where bears, by no means fierce and exceedingly good to eat, are to be found, as are also the savory wild duck and other varieties of game. The islands are covered with trees; chestnuts, walnuts, apples and plums abound; and in season the wild vines are heavy with grapes of which the forest rangers say they have made a wine that considering its newness, was not at all bad.*[2]

But since its first European settlement, Detroit has been a place to be conquered and its resources claimed. In the early 1700s, Europeans thought the land was theirs for the taking, so all commodities obtained were counted, measured and priced in the name of their sovereign. Beaver pelts were put under a monopoly for the French king; the beaver itself became an object of capitalism. Years went by, and after the War of 1812, the Michigan territory was declared property of the United States with the signing of the Treaty of Ghent in 1814.

After one hundred years of meager European settlement—traders, trappers and pioneers alike—a small port was built to accept provisions for the community there. In 1796, Lieutenant Colonel John Francis Hamtramck sailed to this small Detroit port, which existed at the time by the foot of Washington Boulevard. He arrived just two days after the *Swan*, the first ship to fly the American flag on the Great Lakes.[3] Records indicate Hamtramck was only five feet, five inches tall, and his letters composed to various generals and colleagues show that he lacked good grammar and spelling, probably because English was not his native tongue.[4] Despite this, he was an able general who had not only been given command over several forts along the Wabash River in Indiana and Ohio but was also in charge of the fort in Detroit and helped to establish Fort Dearborn in Chicago.[5] He purchased a plot of land just outside Detroit and has thus unknowingly made himself immortal. He died in 1803, just a few years after his purchase, and was buried at Ste. Anne de Detroit. He was later reinterred to a commemorative grave site at the veterans' memorial in downtown Hamtramck. Though he only spent six years splitting his time between Detroit and Fort Wayne before his death, the city of Hamtramck now bears his name.

The predominantly Polish neighborhood established in an area just south of Hamtramck developed slowly until the turn of the twentieth century. In the late 1800s, it was a sparsely settled community and was considered rural compared to the inner parts of Detroit. Much of Detroit consisted of ribbon farms. Long, narrow strips of land, which instead of expanding outward in a wide, square fashion, stretched back into the property in long strips for about a mile or less. One could guess these plots not only provided ample space for more properties (to be sold and bought) but also made property lines easily managed and plotted out, thus eliminating any cause for disputes among neighbors. As industrialization increased, more immigrants flowed into Detroit from all over the world and other parts of the United States seeking relief from various oppressive situations. This is where the journey of the neighborhood known as *Poletown* came to exist. This is the story of the people

Lieutenant Colonel John Francis Hamtramck's grave site at the Hamtramck Veterans' Memorial Park. *Author's photo.*

Lieutenant Colonel John Francis Hamtramck's memorial plaque near the Hamtramck Veterans' Memorial Park. *Author's photo.*

who lived and worked in the neighborhood and the story of the people who fought for its continued existence. This is the story of an unforgettable priest and his adamant fight to save the church for his parishioners, even though the stress of it has been rumored to have cost him his life. This is the story of Poletown told through the eyes of those who witnessed its passing.

THE LOST NEIGHBORHOOD

A History

Poletown: What's in a Name?

Around 1880, Detroit was on its way to becoming a modern city with a lot of employment opportunities. Many migrants hated the menial jobs they obtained in other industrialized areas of the country. Cities like New York, Philadelphia, Boston and Baltimore provided immediate employment in mining coal and factory work, but they were hazardous and didn't pay well. In addition to this, workers were not protected by their employer in any way.

But Detroit! In 1880, Detroit established the Council of Trades and Labor Unions, which later became the Detroit Federation of Labor, an organization created to ensure workers were exposed to safe working conditions and fair wages.[6] In the later years of the nineteenth century, Detroit enjoyed the fruits of industrialization. In 1881, it was the nation's leading stove manufacturer, and the first incandescent lights were used in Metcalf's Dry Goods shop a couple years after and later installed down Woodward and Jefferson.[7] Not only concerned with industry and modernity but also with aesthetics, the city purchased Belle Isle with plans to make it the first island park in the country.

From the late 1800s on, there was a dramatic increase in the population. In 1900, Detroit was the thirteenth-largest city in the country with a population of 285,704.[8] The population had increased by 80,000 individuals in ten years. Naturally, with this influx came the need for efficient public

Image of Belle Isle Horticultural Building around 1910. *Library of Congress.*

transportation. This led to the expansion of families moving into the more "rural" parts of the city. It is here that the diverse neighborhoods of Hamtramck and northeast Detroit began to form. The Polish began to arrive in the 1850s. They found living among their German neighbors comfortable but longed to have a church that spoke Polish. So in 1870, they began to organize their own parish. The groundbreaking for St. Albertus began in the summer of 1872. After this, Poles began to organize and congregate in the neighborhood of Fremont Street and St. Aubin Street. "This migration resulted in the establishment of Detroit's first Polish neighborhood, known among Detroiters as 'Poletown'; to the Poles, however, it was 'Wojciechowo,' the Wojciech District."[9] Greg Kowalski, a Hamtramck historian, explains that the name *Poletown* originated from a news article published around 1880. A riot broke out between Reverend Dominic Kolasinski of St. Albertus and some parishioners over church records.[10] Because of the commotion of this event—one person was killed—the news reporter(s) dubbed the neighborhood *Poletown* because the people involved were mostly Polish.

But what really centralized the ethnic community of Poletown was the boom of the auto industry and the building of the Dodge Main plant. Dodge Main was essential to the shaping of the neighborhood. A new industrial

The Bernard Schwartz plant, site of the cigar factory sit-in strike performed mostly by women in 1937. Poletown was, in many ways, the center of union formation in Detroit. This is one of five cigar factories in Poletown at the time. *Library of Congress.*

Home for the women who worked at the cigar factories. The exterior of the building has fleur-de-lis decorative tiles. It later become the Goodwill Community Church. *Library of Congress.*

Mary and Anthony Zuchinski, first-generation Polish Americans. Hamtramck, Michigan. *Camille and David Turczynski.*

park meant more jobs, so many immigrants and native residents flocked. Businesses emerged to supply the growing area with dry goods, bakeries and cafés. With this, other necessities like schools, churches and hospitals appeared. St. Joseph's Hospital, for example, first established under the name Samaritan Hospital, was built two years after Dodge Main opened.

Safety in Numbers

Many Poles and other ethnic communities, including Germans, Romanians, Austrians, Albanians and Chaldeans, all lived and worked together in Poletown. Even though they were essentially American citizens, Poles still experienced prejudice. For years, they struggled to get jobs. "Signs in storefronts read, 'Poles need not apply.' The German building, St. John's Church, said the Poles could help pay to build the church but would have to sit in a segregated balcony. Company managers assigned Poles to the dirtiest and most dangerous factory jobs, forcing them to work ten-to-twelve-hour days, six days a week."[11]

There was a stigma against Poles especially because of their religion. According to Jim Jaczkowski, a former resident of Poletown East, the prejudice centralized on Catholicism. "The immigrants in the United States were basically Anglo-Saxon, so they were Protestant. Even when the Germans came through in the 1830s and 1850s, they were mostly Lutheran. When the Slavs came in—the Polish, the Russian—they were Roman Catholic. People were afraid of it. It offended some people. The priests dressed in garbs, walked around with monstrances, and the churches they built up—people felt threatened."[12] Even Leslie Tentler, professor of history at the University of Michigan–Dearborn, echoes this. In her book *Seasons of Grace*, Tentler wrote that the Catholic Church was "stigmatized as a foreign institution, out of sympathy with American values."[13] Anyone studying American history would see this has been a trend since the country's beginning. Ethnic groups that seemed "out of sympathy with American values" usually did experience some form of prejudice; sadly, in some cases this prejudice continues today. But what were American values one hundred years ago? Protestant. English. White. Everyone else was left to fend for themselves. So what did immigrants do? They banded together in little enclaves around the country where they could feel accepted by their neighbors and "blend in" in their own communities and neighborhoods. They created communities that represented their culture and heritage and perhaps even kept their languages alive.

Some might say the prejudice against Poles continues today. In emails sent back and forth among guests of the 2002 *Quo Vadis* (Where are you marching) *American Polonia?* in Orchard Lake, Michigan, statements discussing "propagandized Non-Poles" expressed this continued frustration. "Polonia is the most dumb-down ethnic group in the entire world," one member wrote. "We are unique in this respect. Everywhere, we are at the bottom rung in a society. We have the worst self-image."[14]

In November 1970, Polish residents of Detroit picketed the *Detroit Free Press* for running a cartoon titled "Look Out! Polish Wedding!" Finding the cartoon offensive, forty Polish Americans picketed outside the *Free Press* building chanting, "We are Polish, and we are proud." They presented a bouquet of red and white flowers to the editors. The flowers, they said, symbolized the blood of Polish freedom and peace patriots. "There are 650,000 Polish Americans in this city," said Polish American folk teacher Michael Krolewski. "This kind of thing has to stop right now."[15]

Although there were other ethnic groups living there, the Polish community in Poletown seemed to be the most prominent considering the surrounding businesses and overall accessibility for new Polish migrants. From 1910 to 1999, the Halicki Travel Agency on Chene Street helped migrants, particularly Polish, assimilate. Walter Halicki, the founder, exchanged foreign currency and arranged trips from Europe to America and back. His collection of over eighty thousand passenger tickets and other documents can be found in the Burton Historical Collection at the Detroit Public Library.[16]

The Polish population grew to such an extent that Poles sought to build Polish Roman Catholic churches. With their numbers, they could finance much of the building out of their own pockets. In her study of the history of the Archdiocese of Detroit, Leslie Tentler explained, "Life was centered in the neighborhood on its institutions and its influential men. The priest was naturally the dominant figure in the community, a leader in secular as well as religious matters and the church was a community center in the widest possible sense."[17]

With this mentality in mind, it is easy to see why in 1981, many of the older existing Polish residents fought so hard to save not only their neighborhood but also the Immaculate Conception Catholic Church, the only Polish Roman Catholic church within the 465 acres slated for demolition.

Newspapers and advertisements were written in Polish to accommodate the ever-increasing Polish community. According to a Social and Ethnic Historical Report conducted on behalf of the William Kessler Architectural Firm in 1980, the anonymous author states, "An indicator of this growing ethnic [Polish] power is seen in the building of the neighborhood's second school in 1913. Built on the block bounded by Lyman, Trombly, St. Aubin and Dubois, the school was named in honor of Joseph F. Majeski, a prominent member of the Polish community, and supporter of St. Albertus Church and the Polish Century Club. The fact that in the twelve years from the naming of Parke school, the Poles had gathered sufficient political strength to have a school named for one of their own, is significant."[18]

The Smigielski family moved into the neighborhood in the 1940s and established a funeral home. "Growing up we had German families, Polish families and Italian families. They were a mixed group, but they were Americans."[19] John Smigielski said that he didn't remember anyone being blatantly discriminated against. "[Poles] spoke Polish—that was their language, so they associated with each other. The grocery store owners knew several different languages so they could communicate. [At home] you used Polish, but you only used it to keep your kids in the dark," he added with a chuckle.[20]

Jim Jaczkowski explained that when his father came to the Poletown neighborhood, he did not know English. "He came over with fifty cents in his pocket. He couldn't speak English. People discriminated against [the immigrants] because they couldn't speak English. In my house, my mom wouldn't let my grandfather speak Polish to me. 'Tata,' she'd say, 'this is America, you speak English.' When we walked out, he would only speak Polish to me," Jaczkowski remembered.[21]

Polish Traditions Practiced in Poletown

Polish immigrants did not leave their traditions or cuisine in Poland. Many who love pierogi are thankful for this. Especially in a neighborhood predominantly Polish, these traditions were not only shared among neighbors but also churches, businesses, schools and even the newspaper, which advertised popular aspects of Polish culture. Foods like pierogi, gołąbki (stuffed cabbage), kielbasa (sausage) and kapusta (sauerkraut) were eaten by just about everyone. Other dishes like czarnina (duck blood soup) and kluski (homemade noodles) were also made but perhaps not as often today as in the mid-century, when older generations pined for the authentic foods of the old country.

In the Polish tradition, Christmas Eve is *the* celebrated holiday with extended family. It is called *Wigilia*, or vigil. Jim Jaczkowski said this is one of the biggest holidays for Poles. The *żłobek*, the stable with the holy family, would be set out for the Christmas season. The meal for *Wigilia* begins with *opłatek*, a breaking of communion wafer among guests and an offering of fellowship, forgiveness and a blessing for the year ahead. *Wigilia* then continues as a meatless dinner of thirteen dishes to honor the thirteen animals who kept baby Jesus warm at night.[22]

Patricia Siergiej-Swarthout, who grew up in the Poletown neighborhood from 1948 to 1967, said she and her family always celebrated *Wigilia*. Her aunts would come over to help cook along with her older female cousins. After dinner, the family would walk down to the Immaculate Conception Catholic Church, where they would celebrate Christmas Eve Mass at midnight, called *Pasterka*, or the Shepherd's Mass.[23] Patricia grew up in a two-story home on Trombly Street. Her parents, sister, brother and she lived in the main

Celebrating *Wigilia*, 1950s. Patricia Siergiej-Swarthout's family sits around the table. Seated on the left is Patricia's mom and dad with her little sister, Camellia. At the head of the table, toward the back, are Patricia and her uncle, who lived in the upper half of her childhood home along with her grandmother, seated at the opposite end of the table. *Patricia Siergiej-Swarthout.*

part of the home, while her uncle and grandmother lived upstairs. She said Christmas Day was celebrated with just family; her uncle and grandma had their own dinner on that day and would come down to visit.[24]

In addition to *Wigilia*, Easter is also a significant holiday in Polish culture. Jaczkowski said he still gets his Easter basket blessed on Holy Saturday (the Saturday before Easter). This practice is called *święconka*, "the blessing of the Easter baskets." He mentioned that Polish traditions are still practiced in his family. "All of my granddaughters are in Polish dance lessons," he remarked, "and they take Polish cultural lessons, and Polish history is still big in our family."[25] Patricia remembered the blessing of the Easter baskets too. Her mother would place lamb-shaped butter in the basket along with eggs and holy water, and then she'd place the basket in the aisle for the priest to come by and bless it.

John Smigielski, whose family owned Smigielski Funeral Home in Poletown, mentioned that he, too, enjoyed many of the traditional Polish foods such as gołąbki, sweet bread, kielbasa and pigs in a blanket. He remembered they usually ate pierogis on Friday, and they were either cheese- or kapusta-

The interior of Immaculate Conception during the Christmas season. *Patricia Siergiej-Swarthout.*

Patricia Siergiej-Swarthout pictured with her mother and little sister on Easter morning, 1950s. They are carrying their Easter baskets to be blessed at Immaculate Conception Catholic Church in the Polish tradition of *święconka*. *Patricia Siergiej-Swarthout.*

filled. He mentioned they always had cabbage and herring around, as well as homemade horseradish. "My dad used to sit on the back steps," he said, "and grind his own horseradish, and his eyes were as red as beets, crying. He would make his own kielbasas. That's what you did—you packed and canned. Every basement had stoves and sinks and countertops so you could can food in your basement. You didn't take it all upstairs because you didn't have room. Those were living quarters. So, you have bedrooms and kitchens and bathrooms. As things progressed, maybe you got a shower with a curtain around."[26] He laughed.

NEIGHBORHOOD LANDMARKS

Dodge Main

John F. Dodge and Horace E. Dodge began building and supplying drivetrains for Ford motor cars in 1903.[27] A drivetrain is the system of movable components on the underside of a vehicle that consists of the axles and bars that connect tire movement to the steering wheel. When Henry Ford established the Henry Ford Company in 1901, his wage policy of five dollars a day no matter your skin color or ethnicity convinced many to join his assembly line. This created a great migration to Detroit.[28] Ten thousand men, for example, waited outside the Ford plant on Woodward Avenue in Highland Park, Michigan, on a blistering cold morning in 1914. Men started lining up at 3:00 a.m. and continued to swarm the gates until they opened at 7:00 a.m. that morning.[29]

With the invention of the automobile and its affordability, not to mention accessibility to an expanding middle class, there came an increase in entrepreneurs who decided to take on the lucrative venture themselves. The Dodge brothers did just that. By the late nineteen aughts, their business was so good that they outgrew their factory and built the Dodge Main plant on the southern edge of Hamtramck.

Dodge Main was essential to the shaping of Poletown and Hamtramck. A new industrial park meant more jobs, so many immigrants and native residents flocked to the new plant. Businesses emerged to supply the growing neighborhood with grocers and cafés. Between 1910 and 1920, the

Aerial view of Dodge Main and surrounding Poletown neighborhood. *Library of Congress.*

population in the whole of Wayne County increased by 200,000 individuals, according to the historical records of the U.S. Census Bureau.[30] By this time, much of Chene Street was commercial, supplying the necessities to the neighborhood.[31] In a nostalgic article published in the *Detroit News* in 1985, Douglas Ilka wrote, "Many immigrants worked their entire lives at Dodge Main without learning English. An eye chart on the plant doctor's wall featured a picture of a cat. If an immigrant could recognize the cat by saying the word 'meow,' the plant had another employee."[32]

Dodge Main opened in 1910 and drew immigrants to its gates from all over the world. "By 1920 Hamtramck's population alone had skyrocketed from 3,559 to 48,615."[33] Bruce Garwood, who grew up in Poletown East, commented that he remembered cars rolling off the assembly line when he was a kid in the 1950s. "I clearly recall how they would test drive 1955 and 1956 Dodge automobiles right down Joseph Campau Street. The cars were beautiful colors in those days—a lot of two-tone cars. And at times they would stop suddenly to test the brakes, etc. This was living in the Motor City at its best."[34]

St. Joseph's Hospital

Around 1912, after the Dodge Main plant opened, a group of physicians saw the growing population centering itself around the plant and decided a hospital would be a helpful addition. In the late summer of 1913, the Samaritan Hospital opened its doors on East Grand Boulevard and Milwaukee. It had the capacity to host as many as fifty patients. In 1916, a fourteen-bed addition was built. And in March 1923, it was purchased by the Sisters of Mercy from Dubuque, Iowa. The day the purchase agreement was to be signed, four sisters waited all day at the Detroit train station for a ride to the hospital. Apparently, there was a delay in the purchase agreement, and they did not make it to the hospital until nightfall.[35] When the first child was born that night and baptized by Sister Mary Lourdes, the hospital's first administrator, the event was marked and celebrated. "Thus, too, was born another commitment by the Sisters of Mercy."[36]

In 1924, the architectural firm Maguolo and Quick was given the task of designing the 125-bed, four-story addition.[37] The following year, the League of Catholic Women published an article detailing the interior and exterior architecture of the building:

> *The new building is strictly fireproof being of a reinforced concrete skeleton design enclosed with brick walls. It is constructed of a rough texture with an Indiana limestone base up to the first-floor windows, and stone bands and trim above this point. The main entrance is on the boulevard side. This entrance is a plain, dignified, arched opening in a rusticated stone bay, with a carved stone rope mold carried around the opening.*
>
> *The floors of the vestibule, lobby and lobby stair hall are of colonial gray marble, and the walls of these rooms are of McMullen gray marble laid in an ashlar pattern. The lobby is octagonal in plan with a low vaulted ceiling of antique plaster divided into eight segments by low relief plaster band ornaments.*
>
> *The opening off the lobby is a waiting room, information room, public office, stair hall, office doors and a niche with a statue of Saint Joseph.*
>
> *On the first, third, fourth and a part of the second floors are located the private rooms and baths, with a diet kitchen, utility rooms, sunrooms, nurses' stations, scrub and linen rooms....Most of the [patient] rooms [are] furnished with a private bath and toilet. The chapel and quarters for the chaplains are also located on the first floor.[38]*

Shortly after operations began in the new addition, the sisters realized the necessity for nurses' and nuns' quarters. They commissioned Detroit architectural firm Donaldson and Meier to build a nurses' home across the street, complete with a tunnel that ran under East Grand Boulevard to connect the home directly to the hospital.[39] The historic firm built other landmark buildings around Detroit, including the David Stott Building, Sacred Heart Seminary, St. Hyacinth Catholic Church (a Polish Roman Catholic church in Poletown East), the Penobscot Building and many other churches and additions to universities in Michigan.

The nurses' home was completed in September 1931 with celebration. Bishop Gallagher dedicated the expansion with a service. Following the ceremony, the guests, who consisted mostly of clergy and nuns, enjoyed dinner together with multiple speakers including the bishop and Detroit mayor Frank Murphey.[40]

For almost seventy years, St. Joseph's Hospital administered to the neighborhood and beyond, caring for many immigrants, some of whom could not speak English. In the case of a Polish-speaking patient, there were two Polish-speaking priests in the area, Father Cendrowski of Immaculate Conception and Father Karasiewicz, the "iron priest of Poletown," who would eventually fight to save Immaculate Conception when the neighborhood was razed for the General Motors assembly plant, in which case the hospital and nurses' home were also demolished. "When the hospital finally closed [in 1981 to make room for the GM plant], close to eighty patients were moved out of its facilities, some returned home, others were transferred to St. Joseph's renovated quarters on Clinton Street in downtown Detroit, and women about to give birth had to be transported to Hutzel hospital."[41] So the neighborhood said farewell to a beautifully built structure, another masterpiece of Detroit's architectural history in both the nurses' home and the hospital itself, destroyed in the name of progress.

Beth Olem Cemetery

In the middle of the General Motors Detroit/Hamtramck Assembly Plant parking lot stands an imprisoned cemetery. Only open to the public twice a year, the Beth Olem Cemetery or the Smith Street Cemetery is host to 1,100 Jewish graves. The trees that grow there are as old as the graves

Image of Jewish graves in Beth Olem cemetery. *Author's photo.*

themselves. It is strange to see them today shooting out of the concrete parking lot within the fenced lot of the plant. Standing erect and out of place, they are protected by a deteriorating brick wall amid a concrete paradise. The only thing invading the protected cemetery now is the beautiful yet invasive grove snail, which seems to have made its home on just about every moss-covered grave.

The cemetery was first plotted in 1862. Sam Fleishman and Isaac Parchelsky purchased the 1.0-acre lot in their own names, and after years of adding additional plots, the entire space ended up being closer to 2.2 acres.[42] As the area became more industrialized, the Jewish community relocated north, leaving behind their cemetery.[43] It is considered one of the only Jewish memorial parks within the city limits of Detroit. The last body was buried there in 1948.

In 1966, around the time Chrysler took over the Dodge brothers' plant, the corporation purchased the surrounding property of the cemetery to use for parking.[44] When they did this, they closed the original entrance of the cemetery but opened one on Clay Street. When GM took over, Clay Street itself was wiped off the map, leaving only a gravel pathway to the entrance of the cemetery where guests could park and walk through the Beth Olem entrance. Unfortunately, plot records for the cemetery have gone missing,

Image of the Beth Olem Cemetery entrance. *Author's photo.*

but in 1975, Congregation Shaarey Zedek conducted a count of the marked graves and determined there were around 733 headstones.[45]

Because of Halachic Law, which includes strict rules as to how bodies of the deceased should be treated and buried, the graves could never be moved as the hands of ownership passed over the area. So the graveyard sits eternally imprisoned by concrete.[46]

Now the assembly plant has a guide stationed to show guests where to go and where to park when they visit the cemetery. Its entrance is an opening under an ornate archway painted an earthly green that is beautiful but seems to fade into the scenery as if to go unnoticed. The chapel that once stood in the middle of the cemetery was torn down in 1982 because it had deteriorated beyond repair. In city maps made before the razing of the neighborhood, the chapel is still visible. Visitors will notice its massive void as they enter the space, which looks more like a natural aisleway between the west side of the cemetery and the east. When asking people from the old neighborhood about the cemetery, many were unaware of its existence. John Smigielski, the embalmer and funeral director at his family's funeral home, only recalled the B'nai David Jewish Cemetery along Van Dyke on Detroit's East Side, nearly neglected and forgotten until its clean-up in 2016. Larry Geromin, who grew up north of Poletown, said he used to visit the Beth Olem Cemetery at night with his friends. "We were probably fourteen, fifteen, sixteen....We used to walk around and read tombstones."[47] He admitted that the place was exciting to visit because at that age it felt spooky, especially at night, and it gave him and his friends something to do. Its obscurity is probably the result of the cemetery being in the north end of the neighborhood, which was mostly industrial. Although Clay Street was the road to take if you were heading toward the well-traveled Joseph Campau Street, it seems to have faded in the memories of most.

Hervey C. Parke School

In 1901, the Hervey C. Parke School was opened on Milwaukee and East Grand Boulevard. The school was named after Hervey Coke Parke, the president and treasurer of the pharmaceutical company Parke, Davis & Co., which is now known as Pfizer. In 1920, it became known as one of the first Detroit schools to practice platooning.[48] Platooning was a teaching method

Front of Hervey C. Parke School. *Library of Congress.*

Back of Hervey C. Parke School. *Library of Congress.*

similar to what high schoolers and middle schoolers experience today, in which students switch teachers every hour or so depending on the subject. The location continued its existence as an elementary school until it was razed for the GM plant. It was destroyed by fire, a result of the rampant arson committed in the neighborhood that summer of 1981.

John F. Majeski School

John F. Majeski was a Polish immigrant and a prominent member of the Poletown community. He was a member of St. Albertus Catholic Church and a supporter of the Polish Century Club.[49] The building, constructed in 1913, was mainly used as an apprentice school, as the area was highly industrial. In the 1920s, it began an elementary school program for the surrounding neighborhood. In the 1930s and '40s, however, its many windows made it a perfect building for use as an open-air sanatorium for tuberculosis patients.

John F. Majeski School. *Library of Congress.*

Immaculate Conception

The Immaculate Conception Parish is able to confront the financial burden but needs temporary help.... With employment things may improve rapidly, but at present the parish must have a moratorium.
— *Father Bortnowski, priest of Immaculate Conception,*
January 3, 1932[50]

Designed in 1919 and finally erected in 1928, the plans and execution of Immaculate Conception did not come without its mishaps. Any student of U.S. history knows that in 1929, the stock market crashed, which left many people broke and later without work as we entered what is now known as the Great Depression. The years 1932 and 1933 were considered the hardest as unemployment rose to 25 percent. But no one could have foreseen this economic tragedy in 1919 when Father Bortnowski received permission from the Archdiocese of Detroit to build a church and rectory for the Polish population in the neighborhood. He received "an option on

Exterior of Immaculate Conception. *Library of Congress.*

the five lots located on Dane Avenue at Moran Avenue, and the five lots on Trombly Avenue at Moran Avenue."[51] Early in 1920, the plans for the church were approved and eventually completed in 1928 under the initiation and supervision of Father Bortnowski. It was built to hold a capacity of 916 seated individuals.[52] But it seems the Immaculate Conception began its history coiled in a legal battle with the contractor. Records show Father Bortnowski requested several last-minute revisions to the design, which the contractor couldn't fulfill. Letters written from the contractor are riddled with both defiance and unwavering pride as Father Bortnowski was blamed for all the delay and mistakes in the work. "Father Bortnowski at first wanted Byzantine style, then Romanian, Soloniki, etc., etc., ending with Beuron Style. After the exterior plans were made[,] he decided that the ornamental column cap, etc. be of pure Egyptian Styles."[53]

"The style," Bortnowski argued, "was agreed upon on June 9th, 1927 and never have I changed one single thing, on the contrary, I had insisted on not deviating from the accepted Beuron Style."[54]

Interior of Immaculate Conception, with view of entrance. *Library of Congress.*

Payments then began to wane, and in January 1932, when the economic crisis got worse, a letter written from loan officer M.F. Ryan to Monsignor Doyle, the auxiliary bishop of Immaculate Conception, complains about the debts owed and calls the situation "a very deplorable condition."[55] He commented that, "This mortgage was made January 10, 1928 and Father Bortnowski has not paid anything on account of the principal during the term of the loan. It would seem to me that in four years he ought to husband some funds to make some payment on the principal."[56] Many Detroit churches suffered at this time, sacrificing, in the midst of construction, limestone, brickwork and stained glass just to keep the parish going in the years of the Depression.

In 1932, the debts for Immaculate Conception were finally paid, but it was only possible with a loan from the archdiocese. Then, after this immense undertaking and the perseverance to see his plan through, Father Bortnowski was removed from his position at Immaculate Conception. "I will obey the order of my Rt. Rev. Ordinary, but I have the duty to stand

Above: Interior of Immaculate Conception, with view of altar. *Library of Congress.*

Opposite: Immaculate Conception church bulletin printed in Polish. *Hamtramck Public Library.*

for my honor and my good name, the only valuables I possess," he wrote. In a letter to the auxiliary bishop, Monsignor Doyle, the parishioners wrote, "The news of the removal of our dear pastor Rev. Dr. Stanislaus Bortnowski from the pastor-ship of the Immaculate Conception parish, has indeed filled our hearts with grief."[57] They added, "[We] express our sincere regret and sorrow, begging Your Excellency to alter your decision and retain our good pastor."[58]

When the economy recovered from the Depression, the church began to experience fruitful years. The parishioners at Immaculate Conception held fast to the Polish traditions and the Polish language. Its Masses were held in Polish, and its bulletins were also in Polish. Parishioners often gathered for Polish celebrations and holidays. "People were all neighbors or all friends. If they had a fight, they wouldn't go to court; they would go to the rectory," said Poletown resident Clara Sieczkowski.[59] "Some of these families," said

1

LITURGIA MSZY ŚWIĘTEJ

ŚPIEW I PROCESJA WEJŚCIOWA   **WSTAĆ**

SERDECZNA MATKO, Opiekunko ludzi,
Niech Cię płacz sierót do litości wzbudzi.
    Wygnańcy Ewy do Ciebie wołamy:
    Zmiłuj się, zmiłuj, niech się nie tułamy.

Do kogóż mamy wzdychać nędzne dziatki?
Tylko do Ciebie, ukochanej Matki:
    U której Serce otwarte każdemu,
    A osobliwie nędzą strapionemu!

Zasłużyliśmy, to prawda, przez złości,
By nas Bóg karał rózgą surowości;
    Lecz kiedy Ojciec rozgniewany siecze,
    Szczęśliwy, kto się do Matki uciecze.

     K. W imię Ojca i Syna i Ducha Świętego.
     L. Amen.

POZDROWIENIE

K. Miłość Boga Ojca, łaska Pana naszego Jezusa Chrystusa i dar
    jedności w Duchu Świętym niech będą z wami wszystkimi.
L. I z duchem twoim.

K. Przeprośmy Boga za nasze grzechy, abyśmy mogli godnie
    odprawić Najświętszą Ofiarę.

Po krótkim milczeniu wszyscy razem wyznają grzechy:

L. Spowiadam się Bogu wszechmogącemu i wam, bracia i
    siostry, że bardzo zgrzeszyłem myślą, mową, uczynkiem i
    zaniedbaniem: moja wina, moja wina, moja bardzo wielka
    wina.
    Przeto błagam Najświętszą Maryję zawsze Dziewicę, wszy-
    stkich Aniołów i Świętych i was, bracia i siostry, o mod-
    litwę za mnie do Pana Boga naszego.
K. Niech się zmiłuje nad nami Bóg wszechmogący i odpuściwszy
    nam grzechy, doprowadzi nas do życia wiecznego.
L. Amen.

Father Matlenga in an interview with Marco Trbovich for the *Detroit Free Press* in 1973, "originally mortgaged their homes to finance the building of this church (Sweetest Heart of Mary). Father Bogulaus Ponanski, pastor at Sweetest Heart of Mary rhetorically asked the reporter, 'How many people would do that today? And if a man wanted to would his wife allow him? Or vice versa? Today if that happened, it would make the news.' Back then, it was a common practice."[60]

WHAT THE CHILDREN
OF POLETOWN REMEMBER

Candy Kitchen

David Wronski maintains a blog called *Wronski Wrambles*, where he talks about his life with a few posts dedicated to his childhood in Poletown. "When I was a boy," he wrote in a blog post titled "Candy Kitchen,"

> *Poletown was my hood. And a certain candy shop was my church of sweet refuge. There are so many other deeply felt and precisely recalled memories of that neighborhood. But I want to remember one that was for me, as a boy, an integral part of the richness of life, and particularly so during the Easter season: The Candy Kitchen.*
>
> *The Candy Kitchen of my youth is gone. I don't know if it closed when the owners retired, but I do know that it is buried somewhere under the Cadillac Poletown factory* [General Motors Hamtramck/Detroit Assembly Plant]. *It was located on a corner at the intersection of Chene and Trombly streets.*[61]

In an interview, he recalled "vividly going from East Grand Boulevard, trudging through the snow, fresh snow [at night], going for a banana split, and sitting at the candy kitchen all alone."[62] His wife painted an abstract picture of this ethereal memory for David.

In an excerpt from his post about his beloved Candy Kitchen, he described the interior in extraordinary detail:

Inside was a huge space with a high tin paneled ceiling and floors covered in those old fashioned glazed ceramic hexagonal white tiles with black borders and accents. On the right as you entered were the oak and beveled glass cases filled with an assortment of all types of handmade chocolate bonbons. On top of the cases and on the shelves in back were huge jars filled with a rainbow of colorful sugary treats. One jar that I visited often was the one with rock candy. One of my favorite fascinations, rock candy, translucent crystals of pure sugar formed around thin white strings. How'd they do it?

The back of the store was separated by a white lattice gazebo style partition. Potted palms, here and there. In the center back there were tables and along the walls, booths painted white and in the same gazebo motif. I never ever saw anyone sitting there, and I imagined there were ghosts from an earlier time when bobbysoxers would come in after school and hang out nursing a soft drink and listening to bebop on the jukebox. The kind with the real bubble lights and actual vinyl discs. Or, in an even earlier time, when a fella would take his gal for a date and linger over a shared milkshake with two straws and some innocent flirtation.

Candy Kitchen painting by Michele T. Fillion. *Michele T. Fillion and David Wronski.*

On the left side of the shop in front was a small showcase with packaged items such as gums and Life Savers and such and the cash register. But the crown jewel of the whole shebang was the soda fountain. About eight or so floor-mounted high stools set before a bar of solid swirled gray marble. Right behind was the usual wet bar set up replete with sweet condiments and syrupy flavorings. Naturally, there was a fancy dispenser tap with plain water and fizzy soda. Not the flavored soda like now, just (2 cents) plain seltzer. The syrups were added to order.

And, finally, up against the wall an elaborate carved wood built-in of dark mahogany done in the art nouveau style. A counter set up with glassware, a milk shake blender, and a dispenser of malt powder for those malted milkshakes. Straws and the ever-present jar of footlong pretzel sticks. And behind it all, three large expanses of mirrors framed in finely carved wood. A palace. An altar.[63]

Home Theater and Iris Theater

When asked about the Candy Kitchen per David Wronski's memory, Patricia recalled that it was probably the candy shop near the Home Theater where she would walk to see a show. She remembered they used to give out dinner plates, which seemed to be a memorable incentive to entice repeat customers. "Back then you could get a set of plates or bonus coupons if you came to the theater three days a week," remembered John Smigielski. "On Saturday, it'd be an all-day event. You'd get two or three movies and the serials that were being put on the screen, so the next Saturday you'd have to come back to see the next chapter. *Batman* or the *Lone Ranger* or *Flash Gordon*."[64] On the social website *Water Winter Wonderland*, a place where Michigan folks can share their various Michigan memories "past and present," one visitor to the page memorializing the Home Theater or the New Home Theater remembered when her parents took over the theater in the mid-1960s and converted it into a teenage nightclub, calling it The Castle thereafter; it was also a venue for local bands. One contributor mentioned the last band name on the marquee was the Puzzled Corner Band until the building was razed for GM.[65]

The same website talks about the Iris Theater, on the corner of Chene and East Grand Boulevard. From 1916 to 1954, it operated as a single house theater. It went out of business in 1954 and was unoccupied until the Detroit Theater Organ Club used it for a year in 1961. It then sat vacant until 1970, when it was torn down.[66]

Potato Chip Central

It seems Poletown residents and perhaps the entire baby boomer generation loved potato chips. There were about fourteen different manufacturers and distributors of potato chips in Detroit alone in 1943, many of them near Hamtramck and Poletown. Bruce Garwood, who lived in Poletown East, worked at a candy shop just south of I-94. He said potato chips were a hot seller in the '50s and '60s. The candy store at which he worked was called Homemade Candies and was run by a German couple. Garwood remembered they specialized in candy apples, which sat on the checkout counter to entice customers along with potato chips—the other hot commodity.

Larry Geromin, who grew up in Hamtramck, said he used to walk to the Hamtramck park. On the way was a store where kids could get a free bag of freshly made potato chips.[67] This salty snack seems to be in the memory of most Poletown and Hamtramck residents back then. Camille and Dave Turczynski, who grew up in Hamtramck at the time, shared a similar memory of not only chips but also bottles of Towne Club soda to wash them down.

Patricia remembered her dad often brought home boxes of Better Made potato chips. Along with the snack came little dishes for individual helpings, which Patricia remembered looked a lot like coffee filters. One year she gave the tasty treat up for Lent, and at the Easter church service, she remembered being so excited for the fasting season to end so she could enjoy her favorite snack once more.[68]

Roaming the Neighborhood

Beside the Candy Kitchen, Wronski shares many other memories—almost painting the neighborhood store by store. In vivid nostalgic flashes, he remembered in detail:

> *The block just over from the hospital there was a cigarette smoke shop, and there was a little dairy place there. I'd walk and get a chocolate covered ice cream sandwich, or—I was into bike racing—so I'd fill up my tires at the gas station. The Cunningham Drug Store was on the opposite corner, where in my time you could still buy live leeches. The Rexall across the street, was where I often went after school to fantasize over the 8mm and 16mm movie cameras on display. The bank on the other corner*

Chene Street in Poletown looking south. *Library of Congress.*

where I had a savings account, would give me old silver dollar coins for a dollar bill or equivalent; and all nickels were Buffalo Nickels.

The shoeshine shop was down a bit from there, with several seats in a long row. Opposite was a complete setup for hat cleaning and blocking. Men wore hats, you know. Further down, the magazine shop where this young lad would peruse the car magazines and sneak a peek at the covers of the naughty ones too. And, props to that dry goods store where I bought my requisite khaki slacks, and the old Jewish owner would at no extra charge take them apart and resew them in the then current "pegged" style (legs tapered to the bottom).

But now I am recalling another small, but memorable piece of my growing up experience. Perhaps the most mundane.

On Milwaukee, just in from the intersection of Chene Street was the neighborhood shoe repair shop. Over time I made several trips to that funky old place. What I so vividly recall were the sights and smells and sounds. The entire interior of the place looked dark black, brown, like it had been smeared over the years with waxy shoe polish. It smelled of leather, rubber, and an exotic blend of heady aromatics evaporating from glue pots and shoe polish tins.

As you entered, there was a customer counter on the left. Beyond, was a long, continuously running lathe-like spindle on which rotated several types of wheels, each with a dedicated purpose and sound—buffing, smoothing, shaping, sanding, grinding. The whole contraption was run by a large wide leather belt running off an electric motor noisily asserting its presence somewhere out of sight on the floor.[69]

[The Candy Kitchen] was across the street from the Chene and Trombly Lanes where I learned to bowl, when schoolboys worked as pin spotters, and on Friday evenings there was an excellent fish fry on the restaurant menu. And just down a few doors was the barber shop where most of my preteen hair was shorn. I mention that place because of some vivid memories. I recall how it was lined with mirrors on each side of its length. The effect was psychedelic, you could look and see a progression of reflections out to infinity.[70]

"Everybody Knew Everybody"

John Smigielski was born in 1940. His mom and dad bought the funeral home in 1945, just after the war. He lived in the neighborhood until he was married. He said back then in all the neighborhood stores, the store owner or clerk would gather the listed groceries for their customers and would bring them to the counter for purchase. "A lot of the people then trusted each other," he said. "They had a book, so every time you bought something, they'd put your dollar amount in the book, and at the end of the week or the end of the month you'd pay them." He added that neighborhood stores operated that way because everyone knew each other, and this was where the level of trust came from.

"When I was younger," he said, "I had buddies on different blocks, so you could just walk to their house." In Poletown the houses were built close together. If one were to drive down a side street in Hamtramck today, the same effect is preserved there. Neighbor asked neighbor for sugar or flour through open kitchen windows in the summer. After work or supper, families gathered on their porches and shared a conversation with their neighbors over iced tea or some other beverage. Patricia Siergiej-Swarthout remembered it fondly as a "front porch community" where families conversed with one another after supper. Her parents often

Above: Wedding reception of Walter and Genevieve (Jaczkowski) Pielack at the PLAV (Polish Legion of American Veterans) Post 7 on McDougal Street and Kirby Street (Poletown East). *Jim Jaczkowski.*

Left: Catherine Jaczkowski and a relative talk in a backyard in Poletown East (3398 East Ferry Street), Detroit. *Jim Jaczkowski.*

Patricia Siergiej-Swarthout's childhood home, 1950s. Her mother and her sister sit on the stoop watching her father do yardwork. *Patricia Siergiej-Swarthout.*

socialized with her neighbors who sat on their front porch glider when the weather was nice.

Everybody knew everybody was the unanimous statement by former residents who remarked that the neighborhood had a very cozy feeling. If someone needed bread or some other convenience, there were stores on almost every block or just a short walk away. The sidewalks were regularly swept, and the back alleys were kept clean. Shops specializing in individual items sold commodities such as kielbasa, bread and sweets. Stores were accessible on foot, especially on Chene Street where many of the markets were located.

Patricia insisted that the neighborhood was near perfect. She said that the community reminded her of the popular television show *Leave It to Beaver*. She noted that parents never seemed worried when the kids played outside. There was never any reason to fear anyone because "everybody knew everybody."[71] It was this strong sense of community and knowing who their neighbors were that produced this feeling of security and safety. Patricia said, as a child, she often left the house at nine o'clock in the morning and didn't come home until lunch. Her parents never worried because the neighborhood felt safe and the neighbors watched out for one another.[72]

The phrase "everybody knew everybody" was echoed again by Darlene Zabrzenski of St. Hyacinth Catholic Church in Poletown East. Darlene has been attending St. Hyacinth and working as its secretary for a combined seventy years. "The area was a family associated area. We had bakeries here, we had hardware stores. You'd sit on the front porch; you'd wave to people passing by. It was just a happy family area." Father Poznanski of Sweetest Heart of Mary described life in Poletown as "culturally rich, self-contained, and self-sufficient."[73]

For fun, kids rode their bikes up and down the street and played baseball in the alleys because, as David Wronski remembered, "they were spotlessly clean." Wronski lived in the neighborhood around the same time as Patricia and described a similar carefree childhood. In his youth, Wronski said he and his friends walked everywhere. "We'd prowl the neighborhood....We were big on radios, so I'd take my portable radio and walk around listening to music."[74]

Wronski, born in 1943, grew up in Poletown near St. Joseph's Hospital and St. John the Evangelist Church. His mother was a homemaker, and his father was a factory worker at the Dodge Main plant. David said his father "was very dutiful, and always on time."[75] His parents had a four-family flat; they lived there until he was in college, when they moved to a place on East Grand Boulevard.

Present-day St. Hyacinth Roman Catholic Church. *Nina Ignaczak.*

Jim Jaczkowski, who grew up between Mount Elliot and Moron on East Kirby, remembered it was like living in a different country. "Everybody spoke Polish. Everybody knew the butcher, the baker and the candlestick maker, and everybody had their own parish to go to. At one time, there were seven to eight Polish churches there." He mentioned people would choose which church to go to based on boundary lines, but they might also choose a certain church because of the priest.

Choir Kids and Altar Boys at Immaculate Conception

Patricia Siergiej-Swarthout remembered much of her time at Immaculate Conception. She lived down the street from the church where she and her family were parishioners. She said the church was a big part of her life growing up and the heart of the community. In addition to being a parishioner, she went to school there and belonged to the choir. Choir practice was on the mysterious third floor of the church. No one was allowed up there except the choir, but she remembered it was just an attic with some chairs and a piano. In the sanctuary, there was a balcony where the choir sang for Mass. When it came time for Mass, the choir would have to climb a circular staircase and move around the large organ to get to their places. Behind the choir was a room where the church bells, blessed with the names St. John, St. Joseph and St. Sigmunt, rang out an echo of God's voice.

Patricia also attended the Immaculate Conception school and walked home for lunch every day at 11:15 a.m. An hour later, all the children hurried back to school, summoned by a handheld bell the nuns would ring.[76] And in the basement of Immaculate Conception there was a stage concealed behind a heavy velvet curtain where the children would put on plays. In that same basement, potluck parties were conducted complete with Polish dancers.[77] And years later it would host Ralph Nader's attorneys as they fought to save the neighborhood and the church and, after that, the mats of sleeping sit-in protestors, protecting the church from arson, looters and the imminent wrecking ball.

A couple of David Wronski's blog posts are dedicated to his memories of Immaculate Conception Church. "I was an Altar Boy," he remembered. "It was an honor. My mother made sure I would always have an immaculately clean and heavily starched white surplice to wear over my cassock. There's an angelic picture of me somewhere in the attic showing me in that outfit with hands folded in prayer, professionally photographed by one of the local portrait studios on Chene Street. They stopped short of the eyes raised to heaven and the retouched-in halo."[78] Despite this, Wronski explains in his hilariously honest blog post titled "Confessions of an Altar Boy: My Downfall" that he wasn't always the perfect picture of sainthood:

I may have been the only boy to have been kicked out of the Altar Boys. It was on a summer morning during Mass being offered by Pastor Cendrowski. I got sick. I was in a quandary over whether to tell Father, or not interrupt and just leave. I was too shy to interrupt, so I left. Later, he [Father Cendrowski] *sent Dennis Sheida, Dr. Sheida's son, on his Schwinn Phantom to let me know not to ever come back. Talk about a double whammy. Getting kicked out without any recourse; and then there's Dennis on the Phantom anyone would covet. (By the way, seeing his dad, Dr. Sheida, for checkups was a treat. He kept a lower drawer in his desk chock full of candies which he offered kids after visits.) And I got the bad news without explanation. Apparently good Father Cendrowski thought I was being just what he probably thought all boys to be down deep—A BAD BOY.*[79]

Wronski went on to reminisce about the bells of Immaculate Conception:

[They] *were a push button electronic affair. There was a little metal door flush on the right side of the second altar step. Open it and there were five columnar buttons. After Consecration, just before the Elevation of the Host and Adoration, the bells were rung. 1-2-3, 2-3-4, 3-4-5. That was the sequence. Bells was the best. When I got Bells, sometimes I rocked it. Rather than the solemn cadence due for the occasion, I would press them at rocket speed. Thought that was pretty cool. Bing-Bang-Bong…Bang-Bong-Boing…Bong-Boing-Blam!!! Never got called on it. Strange to me even then, because it* did *warrant giving someone a good talking to.*

Wronski said that even the floor tiles at Immaculate Conception were special. "Locally made Pewabic Pottery tiles I suppose. Variegated and with shades of golds, black, browns, umber, copper, orange. Lots of multi-color fading in each tile."[80] The tiles at the Sacred Heart Major Seminary are probably very close to what Wronski remembered. They, too, were made by Pewabic tile, an old Detroit pottery company, in the same color

Example of Pewabic tile in the Sacred Heart Major Seminary, Detroit. *Eric Morgel.*

and around the same time, though the floor at Immaculate Conception was a little more ornate. A hexagonal design was incorporated with these historically significant Detroit tiles.

Wronski then retold a peculiar vivid image that played over in his mind numerous times as a kid: "I recall being at the altar as an altar boy, having this image come to my mind of sledgehammering the altar—the steps to the altar." He went on to say that whether the thought was a premonition or just his own rebelliousness, he didn't know, and he didn't dwell on it, but when the place did come down and people were in fact "sledgehammering the steps," he may have raised an eyebrow or two.

John Smigielski was married in 1963 at the Immaculate Conception Church. "When I was growing up you just walked down the street to Immaculate Conception. They'd have parties, and our family always made their presence known by helping and sponsoring some of the events." His brother and he were in the ushers' club. He said that because they owned the funeral home and funeral homes frequently worked with churches, they made sure they sponsored events and volunteered to keep themselves known within the parish.

From the end of World War II to the late 1950s, the neighborhood was in its prime. Things seemed to buzz right along without pain or strife. People knew one another, the neighborhood was friendly and safe, families were together and the businesses in the neighborhood supplied every need and entertainment the residents could want. Then things began to turn as families sought larger homes in the suburbs with more property. And while the country reeled from events resulting from the civil rights movement and the Vietnam War, the Poletown neighborhood was not immune to the effects as the world turned around its 465 acres, as the reader will see in upcoming chapters.

THE BEGINNING OF THE END

A Highway Runs Through It

Before General Motors razed the Poletown neighborhood, residents had been slowly moving out of the area for decades. The exodus began gradually in the late '50s. Many people argue that the highway systems that cut through the middle of the city enticed people to leave and go to the suburbs. The highways made it easier for people to travel to and from work, but the downside was both I-75 and I-94 divided historic Detroit neighborhoods so that the solidarity of communities became somewhat lost.

Around the mid-1950s, when the last remaining parts of the Black Bottom neighborhood were being leveled for the building of I-75, another major highway, I-94, cut right through what was the Polish epicenter of Detroit. The highway divided the community in such a way that the effects of that divide were still felt when General Motors closed in on the neighborhood in 1981. "That was the first nail in the coffin," Jim Jaczkowski remarked, adding that the neighborhood seemed doomed after that because the community was split apart. "I remember my grandfather lived on Ferry Street, three blocks south of the freeway going in. I would go with him with old wagons and we'd pull lumber out of the old buildings they were tearing down. He would burn it in his boiler. I remember when they started digging the ditches for the freeway and some of my friends and I would take a piece of cardboard and slide down there in winter, like toboggan runs."[81] He went on to explain his theory for why it began to deteriorate the comradery of the neighborhood. "The inability to walk from one place to another limited people, created two different communities—north of the freeway, south of the freeway. After this," he added, "crime increased."

"They cut through Harper Avenue to create I-94," David Wronski remembered, adding that "Father Cendrowski was instrumental getting an overpass at Moran where kids could come from the other side of the expressway and cross over."[82] Of course, the overpass is no longer there. With the lawful use of eminent domain (because the highway would be used for a public purpose), businesses and homes were razed for its construction.

Wronski grew up and lived on East Grand Boulevard near St. Joseph's Hospital. He graduated from the Immaculate Conception School in 1957. He said, thanks to Father Cendrowski and his idea of the overpass, things didn't seem to change much for him as a kid. He mentioned, laughing, that being kids, he and his friends used to throw spitballs off it onto oncoming cars.[83] "We didn't get along very well," he remarked about Father Cendrowski, but he was thankful for the overpass so he could see his friends.

John Smigielski remembered playing on the expressway while it was being built. "When the expressway came through, it chopped up our area—so to speak—divided it from the other areas. So, the neighborhood changed." He went on to say that the neighborhood grocery store was "chopped in half" by the expressway, so residents started to shop at the main grocery store on Chene Street after this. "We'd still had our buddies on the other side of the expressway." Like Wronski, Smigielski was also thankful for the overpass, which made it possible for him to still see his friends.

The Riots of 1967

In the summer of 1967, a blind pig (another word for a speakeasy or illegal bar) was raided by Detroit police. Police dragged both men and women out onto the street and lined them up to conduct arrests. It was reported that a bottle was thrown after word spread that a woman inside was being harassed by the police. Out of this single act of retaliation, it has been said that the infamous '67 riot or rebellion began. Detroit would never be the same. It brought to light the emotions felt by people long silenced by injustice in the city. The violence lasted for five days in July, summoned the national guard and left forty-three people dead and hundreds of city blocks destroyed.

The events that occurred, although emotionally traumatic for the people of Detroit, did not physically affect Poletown, but residents were frightened by it. David Turczynski, a resident of Hamtramck at the time, said he could hear the tanks downtown near the bar on Twelfth Street where the riot began. "We sat on our porches that night, night after night. We could hear gunshots and the tanks rolling down Woodward. *Click-click-click*—with their tracks. We felt we were at war."[84] The country at the time *was* at war. The war in Vietnam had taken many men away from the neighborhood. It seemed to be on the minds of most. Several of the men interviewed for this book were drafted or had fathers or grandfathers who fought in the Second World War. "During World War II alone the area's [Poletown/ Hamtramck] population sent a larger percentage of its own to the armed forces than any other American city. To this day [1987], the city is studded with veteran's clubs."[85]

At the time, Patricia Siergiej-Swarthout worked at IBM downtown. The company simply sent all employees home when word about the violence spread. She remembered the sound of the sirens and saw the smoke floating over from Twelfth Street, which was troubling for her. Her uncle brought home a shotgun, but they did not have to use it. She also remembered smelling smoke from the buildings on fire. The turmoil lasted about a week, but she contemplated canceling her wedding, set for September of that year, because no one knew when the fighting would be quelled.[86]

She said for a week the media reported the news and filmed the events downtown. Although nothing happened in Poletown, she remembered the police constantly monitored the neighborhood.

Larry Geromin, who lived in the northwest part of Hamtramck, said he was in the army at the time, stationed in Germany, but he remembered receiving letters from family members who wrote about the fear they experienced. His brother-in-law sat on their upstairs porch with a shotgun. He said his mother could smell the city burning, and some of the neighborhood kids couldn't go to school because all the schools were closed.[87]

John Smigielski remembered that the violence did not come near Poletown. "We were aware of [the fighting]. Of course, the parents told the kids they had to come in before dark."[88] In addition to this, he mentioned that the parents just made the kids play closer to the house.

Things in Detroit simmered after a week. Patricia went back to work at IBM, the schools reopened and children played once more without their parents worrying.

Holding onto the Roots of Polonia

An activist for Polish freedom from communism for many years, Jim Jaczkowski explained that *Polonia* means "Poles worldwide." Polish communities outside of Poland are considered part of Polonia. The once vibrant Polish neighborhood of Poletown began to empty out after the violence in '67. The population in the Wayne County area had only increased by a few hundred people in a decade.[89] An article about Poletown by the *Free Press* in 1973 reported, "The streets were vibrant with life in an area that is now virtually deserted night and day. Today there is little in Poletown that makes news, save crime."[90] Yet for the Polish who remained in the area, the neighborhood of Poletown was still their comfort zone, despite the rise in crime and what the city was beginning to call *blight*. In another article from the *Free Press* in 1974, Father Kubik of St. Florian Catholic Church said of Hamtramck, "Hamtramck is a small town transplanted in the heart of the city of Detroit. If we were a little town in the heart of a prairie, we'd have been one of the loveliest towns in the country."[91]

Thomas Olechowski, who grew up in the area and still lived there in 1978, prided himself on his political connections in Detroit. He hoped to gain some favor from Detroit mayor Coleman Young and Emmett Moten of the Community and Economic Development Department (CEDD) to create a Polish playland on Chene Street similar to Greektown.[92] "He spearheaded a movement to see Poletown recognized as a distinct and viable ethnic community. His plan for Poletown is based on transforming the Chene street into a Polish-Slavic entertainment strip…complete with 'at least a dozen' ethnic restaurants and bakeries and boutiques."[93] To Olechowski, Poletown was the "cradle of Polish culture in Detroit."[94] Though many in the Polish community doubted he would accomplish such a feat, they applauded his passionate effort.

In 1979, Olechowski organized the Polish Interparish Council to consolidate the Polish identity of the neighborhood. Olechowski showed Emmett Moten the area and Moten agreed that it had potential for revitalization. So when Olechowski saw that another CEDD official was quoted in the *Free Press* as saying that the department had no plans to revitalize the Polish neighborhood, Olechowski became furious and confronted Moten. Even though Moten had the quote pulled from the paper, he confessed to Olechowski that the city had different plans for the area and that instead of seeing its potential to showcase Polonia in Detroit, the neighborhood would be bulldozed for a General Motors plant.[95] "Let me tell you something,"

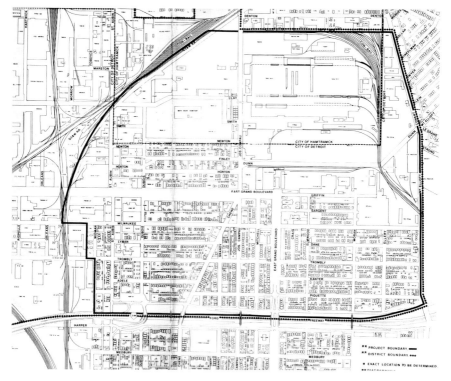

Map of the Poletown area slated for demolition. The solid black line indicates GM's project boundary. *Burton Historical Library.*

Olechowski told a *Free Press* reporter in 1980, "we are the ones who have the roots to attract people back. This is Poletown, and there isn't anything that can change that."[96]

But in fact, there was. Soon after, Olechowski and Richard Hodas—a Poletown resident, an attorney by trade and the vice-chairman of what would eventually be known as the Poletown Neighborhood Council—were invited into Moten's office. There they saw for the first time the architectural plans for the GM plant. "The project was already an accomplished fact. There was just the question about how they [the CEDD] were going to inform the community about it, and that's where they were trying to get our support. Moten thought we were going to work with him. They asked us to get together a list of the quote unquote leaders in the neighborhood to discuss this with. Basically, none of them knew anyone in the area except Tom and me."[97]

The part of the plans Olechowski and Hodas saw as being the most problematic was the plant's small size in comparison to the enormous parcel of land GM wanted. When Hodas expressed this concern, Moten replied that they had no choice, that GM had come to them. Hodas then asked about the churches. "[Moten] kind of shrugged his shoulders and said, 'This is the site that fits the criteria. We have a crisis that has been engendered by General Motors coming to us and threatening to leave. We have to do something.'"[98]

What About the Churches?

Joe Walkowski's body slumped to the scarlet carpet of St. Josephat church with a muffled thud. Father Francis Dolot stopped the Mass. Joe's wife rushed to his side. Parishioners crowded around. It was too late. His heart had failed. Joe was dead. Years later Father Dolot would say there was something almost poetic about Joe's death: something like a blessing that he should die in the church to which he had given so much of his life.[99]

Joe Walkowski was not unlike many of the older Poletown residents passionately devoted to their parish and church life. But by the 1970s, two-thirds of Poletown residents had moved out.[100] Poletown resident Wlodzimierz Nowalkowski argued that even with the absence of many of his old neighbors, he still preferred Poletown over the suburbs even though he recognized the needs of the neighborhood. "This area is very good," he argued, "very comfortable, but it needs a renaissance. I wouldn't want to live in the suburbs. There it's quiet, like village life. People live too much by themselves, separately. I think people who are living here have more communication."[101]

Communication and community were the two essential factors that added to the fervent fellowship and comradery among neighbors. This mentality allowed them to band together when it came time to take on the powers-that-be and make an impact. Those that resisted the General Motors plant are a good example to communities today under the same kind of pressure. Leslie Tentler, author of *Seasons of Grace*, explained that Poles were one of the poorest ethnic groups in Detroit at the time. "They were an isolated group as well, more segregated residentially than any other local population.…Their isolation, coupled with a fierce nationalism bred by oppression in Europe, made them generally suspicious of, and often hostile to, what they regarded as 'outside' authority."[102] And for the Poles, the real authority or dominant figures in their communities were the priests.[103]

St. Nicholas Byzantine Greek Catholic Church on East Grand Boulevard, built in 1924 for a Polish-Slavic congregation. *Library of Congress.*

For many of the older residents in Poletown, community and fellowship centered on the church. Even though church parishioners were dwindling, that sense that the church and its community was a part of home, a part of Polonia or a part of their family was comforting, even for those who had moved to the suburbs. They knew they could always come back to their old church in Poletown, walk down the same aisle they walked as newlyweds or baptized Christians—these were lasting comforts.

John Smigielski found he had to be more flexible with some of Poletown's former residents who came back to use his services for their funerals. "Once in a while, we'd have someone who moved out of the area that decided to come back and patronize us, so we would go to their parishes. It didn't happen often, but it did happen. People had to drive a little bit, had to come to you. Although back then people were a little bit more friendly and supportive."[104]

Immaculate Conception Catholic Church was the only Polish Roman Catholic church in Poletown. But there was also the Holy Trinity Lutheran

Church, which was a Polish Protestant parish, and the St. Nicholas Byzantine Greek Catholic Church, which originally served a Slavic-Polish parish. In addition to these, the neighborhood churches also catered to a number of other sects of Christianity, including the Lutherans, English Roman Catholics, Greek Catholics and Baptists. But church membership began to dwindle after the mass exodus in the 1970s. On a map of Poletown—the area slated for demolition—there are seven visible churches marked out. But what the map does not show are the forgotten storefront churches. However plain they might have been, they still nurtured the community.

There have been many disputes about the number of churches demolished in Poletown. Some sources say there were sixteen churches destroyed. This may have been the case, though some records from storefront churches have been lost. This does not mean there weren't more. As mentioned, many storefront churches were not thoroughly documented. The Roman Catholic churches in Poletown—Immaculate Conception and St. John the Evangelist—were both sold by the archdiocese to the City of Detroit for a total of $2.5 million, but the other churches in Poletown included Temple of Faith Missionary Church, formerly the St. Nicholas Byzantine Greek Catholic Church; Pittman Memorial Church of God in Christ; Holy Cross Church Apostolic Faith; Holy Trinity Lutheran Church; Original Primitive Baptist; Gospel Chapel Church; Greater Baptist Missionary Church; Goodwill Community Chapel; and multiple storefront churches.

When General Motors and the City of Detroit planned the Central Industrial Park Project, they could not have done it without the cooperation of the Archdiocese of Detroit. Cardinal John Dearden was repeatedly criticized not only for selling the churches in the first place but also because the transaction was conducted without consulting the priests or parishioners beforehand. In meetings organized at the beginning of 1980, the archdiocese secretly sold the two churches to the City of Detroit for a little over $1 million each. All evidence of these meetings has disappeared. And of course, the fact that there were meetings involving Cardinal Dearden is merely speculation. But it was known that Cardinal Dearden and Thomas Murphy, the chairman for General Motors, belonged to the same country club, perhaps even golfed together and discussed business affairs. In her book *Poletown*, Wylie made the following observation:

> *Dearden and GM's chairman Thomas Murphy were friends who attended the same exclusive suburban country club, jetted together in private planes, and had the same interests—interests of class. Murphy was a devout*

Catholic who received communion daily. Both he and Dearden frequented the elite Bloomfield Hills Country Club, and Dearden did meet with an association called the Cardinal's Club, a group of prestigious Catholic businessmen convened to honor and meet with the archbishop.[105]

The parish priests of the two churches sold to the city—Father Malcolm Maloney, priest at St. John the Evangelist, and Father Joseph Karasiewicz of Immaculate Conception—received the news of the sale of their churches with shock. They were not a part of the deal, despite Cardinal Dearden's public statement that they were. To this, Father Joe said, "If you were to ask me now the nitty gritty question, 'Is he lying?' In itself, yes. I would say that his statements are lies. To what extent should we accuse him of lying? No, I wouldn't revert to that." Whether the two priests knew about the plan prior to Tom Olechowski or Richard Hodas is unknown. But what's strange is that in April 1980, around the time the city and GM would have been talking about the plans, Cardinal Dearden ordered archdiocese consultors to assess Immaculate Conception in hopes of selling the school building, which Father Karasiewicz had proposed. They agreed to sell the building— an agreement with which Father Karasiewicz was thoroughly involved.[106] The innocent buyer, Riverview Childcare, Inc., did not know the fate of the neighborhood, and there are no records of the transaction after this. So if discussing these matters was a regular occurrence between the archdiocese and the parish priests, why weren't the priests informed about or involved in the very sale that would affect their lives—the sale of their churches?

St. John the Evangelist

St. John the Evangelist Catholic Church began in 1892. Around the turn of the twentieth century, the church boasted about its rich library for the parish youth.[107] Once the population became such that it could build a school, it did so; however, its success was short-lived as the church entered the late 1950s.[108] In the 1970s, St. John's ran into trouble as it tried to rent out its school because the population in the area had dropped to such an extent that it could no longer fill the desks with students.

After the city bought St. John's and Immaculate Conception from the archdiocese to make way for the General Motors plant, both Father Maloney and Father Karasiewicz received a letter from Bishop Krawczak regarding

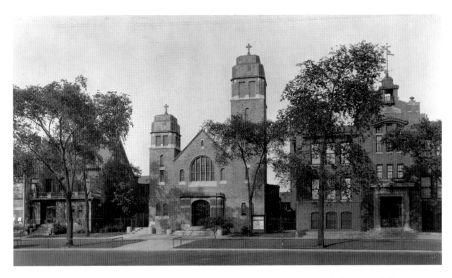

Front of St. John the Evangelist Church on East Grand Boulevard. *Archdiocese of Detroit Archives.*

the sale in February 1981. In her book *Poletown: Community Betrayed*, Jeanie Wylie documents Father Maloney's feeling at this time when his cool manner was compared to that of his outspoken colleague Father Karasiewicz of Immaculate Conception. To this, Father Maloney said he would not feel right about a situation that left his parishioners ill prepared for relocation. "If one group wants to fight the project, if they feel that's necessary, then maybe they can slow things down....I don't want it to look like we're not for the people. It's more complicated than that. What I hate to see is older people at the end of their lives....They shouldn't have to go through all this."[109] He also said that in the beginning he wanted to fight it but felt responsible for his older parishioners. "Nobody just wanted to hand this thing over. But you start playing both sides of the street. I'm a pastor, and I'm responsible for a lot of older people."[110]

At the time, Father Maloney had only been with the parishioners of the church for one year. When the letter came, he quietly obeyed Detroit's archbishop, John Cardinal Dearden, who told him, "You have been in my prayers and continue to be in my prayers."[111] Cardinal Dearden commended the way Father Maloney had handled the situation. The parish organized a "liturgical ceremony and a final social celebration for the closing of the church on May 24th, 1981."[112]

With the eminent domain law, including the quick-take clause, the city could take the land within ten months. Throughout the evacuation, the

St. John parishioners and Father Maloney kept to the city's schedule, only asking for a week's extension to empty the building of all its movable parts. In one of his last letters to Bishop Krawczak regarding the procedure, Father Maloney expressed his concern about vandalism and arson, hoping the church records would soon be secure. He wrote that the Capuchins and the two nuns living on the church property were expected to move out by May 4.[113] Then he went on to say, "At that time I think I will be finding myself a new place to live." Perhaps that was a hint to the archdiocese that it had not yet given him a new assignment, because around the same time, Father Karasiewicz expressed a similar concern that in all their haste to evict him from Immaculate Conception, they had failed to give him a new assignment. He said that was what hurt him the most. "In spite of that notorious day when a group of people came in to boot me out…I would say that I don't think it was intended as such. I think personally that God had blinded them…in their hurry to do what they wanted to do to boot me out. And God had blinded them to the fact that they didn't think about the most primary thing, what to do with *me*.…Not that I care about myself, but normally you would say, 'Well, we'll provide for you' or 'We'll keep in touch with you.' Anything like that."[114]

Father Maloney wrote to the archdiocese requesting assistance to deal with various artifacts, if other churches could use them. He said that someone should be sent to sort through it all, as he could not imagine what one would do with the stations of the cross, for example. He wrote that he had no imagination and perhaps someone would be a better fit to go through the church's belongings. He told the archdiocese that he would need help moving items, especially the heavier ones. "The parishioners who have been helping us so far range in age from sixty-six to eighty-four. Most of them and everyone else who might help have moved out of the area." He ended his letter, dated April 28, 1981, by saying, "Literally I am quite alone and will need some help."[115]

Troubled Times at Immaculate Conception

Trouble started for Immaculate Conception in the 1970s. Due to high property costs, upkeep, dwindling parishioner attendance and meager tithing, the church began to suffer financial trouble. In January 1972, Father Balazy, the priest at Immaculate Conception at the time, sent a letter to Cardinal

Dearden urging him to assist with efforts to find a renter or a purchaser of the school property. He expressed his concern for the financial situation of the parish. "Our school sits empty and yet dwindles our checkbook…. We can only see nothing more than a burden beyond our parish financial capabilities."[116] The Detroit Board of Education even considered the space at one point, but the deal fell through.

Dear Father Balazy,

Cardinal Dearden shares very much the concern expressed in your letter of January 28th for the future of Immaculate Conception Parish. The problem of heavy administrative costs for parishes that no longer make full use of their buildings is one of the problems he has asked me as Vicar of Parishes to try to deal with. As you know, before Monsignor Cendrowski retired, he had great hope that the Detroit Board of Education would lease Immaculate Conception School for this year at least. It is certainly regrettable that the School Board finally reached a decision not to lease your building.
—Bishop Gumbleton, February 7, 1972[117]

The exterior of Immaculate Conception before demolition in 1981. *Patricia Siergiej-Swarthout.*

By November of that year, the church had signed a lease with Project C.H.I.L.D., a daycare and afterschool care program provided at little or no cost for low-income families. In October, the program founders claimed to have no money in their budget to pay the rent since their previous rent at St. John was one dollar a month; however, they said they would be able to pay to maintain the building provided they had a two-year lease. Father Balazy knew this was a bad deal but thought it would provide some income down the road, and at the very least the building would be occupied. Though times were tough for Immaculate Conception, Father Balazy kept his spirits up with the continuation of certain church ministries. In a letter from Bishop Gumbleton to Father Balazy, Bishop Gumbleton sent encouragement: "I notice that in spite of the decrease in income you are still maintaining Christian Service activities including contributions to other parishes. I hope that this kind of giving spirit, even when you are feeling the pinch, will continue to develop in the parish."[118]

Now that the school was occupied, there was the convent to consider. In 1974, the church had 300 families registered, a drop by 174 families from the previous year.[119] The church began looking to lease Immaculate Conception's convent to make up the difference. An offer from a social services program for the mentally handicapped looked promising. "We feel this is a good deal," Father Balazy wrote Bishop Gumbleton. "It will help some neglected needy people and benefit our parish."[120]

In 1976, the church played host to an assortment of ethnic groups. Father Balazy found it difficult to please all these groups while keeping the Polish identity of the church. More important than these concerns was the main outreach focus of the church: to cater to the poor by providing as many funds as they could spare to the Catholic relief service.[121] But by 1977, Father Balazy really had to cut corners. When it became a question whether Project C.H.I.L.D. would continue its lease, Anthony Birnbryer, director of finance and administrative services for the archdiocese, suggested the convent and the school be torn down to eliminate further costs to maintain empty buildings. In June of that year, Father Balazy wrote to Birnbryer that they had had an addition of $3,000 (a thing to be celebrated) to the budget, which was an extra bit of money saved because the church had started handling its own maintenance and laid staff off. "Our parish keeps getting smaller," he wrote, "but we are lucky to have a few good supporters and the strength to do a lot of the work ourselves thus saving for a 'rainy day' which may lie ahead."[122]

Father Joseph Karasiewicz became the priest at Immaculate Conception on August 12, 1979. Early in his time at the parish, Father Karasiewicz advised Cardinal Dearden and the archdiocese to sell the school. On April 15, 1980, he composed a letter stating the reasons for this and advised the archdiocese to take a deal for $75,000 from Riverview Child Care, Inc., instead of waiting for a better offer. In his letter, he reiterated the building's past and its drain on the finances in recent years. In his words:

> The building has a "past." After the closing of the school some eleven years ago, the building was leased on and off for a portion of these past years. Briefly, the leasing brought very little profit, but a goodly amount of grief. The last tenant (Project C.H.I.L.D.—Community Help in Life Development) was literally a "fly-by-night." It disappeared into thin air last August or thereabouts, and has not been seen since, even though it is sought by the State Income Tax Bureau, the I.R.S., and the F.B.I. The building was left, moreover, in disarray....Admittedly, the school building is a "steal" even at the appraised figure. Over the past eleven years, however, there had not been a single cash offer. We cannot afford the possible consequences of dilly-dallying. But in essence, at the heart of the matter, it would be clearly incongruous and downright shameful for us here at Immaculate's to stay in the business of real estate—at the cost of neglecting our primary purpose here—the salvation of souls. Altogether too much priceless time had already been spent on what is for us nothing more than a very costly "white elephant."...The church is primarily a spiritual organization. This is the image we must make. Let it be known at large that the church is willing to make sacrifices, that the church is willing even to "cut off a physical arm"—to save itself spiritually, that the church is not so much concerned with external appearances, as with its primary task—of saving souls.[123]

Father Joseph Karasiewicz as a young priest. *Archdiocese of Detroit Archives.*

But within a few months Cardinal Dearden would sell both the Immaculate Conception Church and St. John the Evangelist out from under those who had worked so hard to keep them running even in their darkest times.

THE POWERS-THAT-BE

Rumor or Truth?

The financial trouble in the churches began because of the unstable economic environment resulting from a mild nationwide recession. In the early 1970s, there was a clear need for jobs, and the city of Detroit sought to clean out some of the blight that had permeated Detroit since the violence of 1967. Vacant houses with broken windows, buildings half burned but still standing and overgrown lots littered with trash were seen all over the city. By 1980, the nation had plummeted into a deeper recession, and the percentage of unemployed seemed willing to sell their very souls, or at least someone else's, for a job.

"A site at I-94 and Mt. Elliott apparently is Detroit's prime candidate for the location of a new General Motors Corp. Cadillac Plant," Michael A. Robinson and Nolan Finley wrote in an article for the *Detroit News* in the fall of 1980. The plant would be a modern facility, mostly automated, but even still GM promised it would provide six thousand jobs to the desperate city. At the time, the city pointed out ten other sites available for the plant, but General Motors liked the one Poletown residents occupied the best, saying "the preparation of the site would be the least costly for the company and pointed out its location in proximity to an essential rail line."[124]

When GM's plan was announced, Patricia Siergiej-Swarthout first heard about it on the news. She remembered feeling immediately sad for her uncle and surprised that the city would or could do such a thing. Her uncle still occupied her childhood home. He was a bachelor. His whole life was the neighborhood, the church, the neighbors, the local pub—these things were a big part of his life.[125]

"So far they are mostly just [rumors]. The city has cased the area, mostly to find out how many homes are on the acreage stretching from old Dodge Main in Hamtramck to the Ford expressway in Detroit, and how many rooms each has.…The work is in the hands of Emmett Moten of the Community and Economic Development Department (CEDD). As of August 18th, no resident had been given an eviction notice. But as the city was trying to find financing to nail down 6,000 jobs…life continues on Trombly," *Free Press* reporter Harry Cook wrote.

> *A motherly lady apologizes for her informal attire, but she is in the midst of washing. Another clips her hedge. Another leans on her garden fence and wonders if she might be able to relocate in Hamtramck. She likes Hamtramck. These are not people who pine for a posh retreat in the suburbs. They are true urban people. They like the bustle of traffic, children shouting in the streets, the sight of people heading for the bus stop with their lunch pails. All they want from life is a small patch of green, a place to set out a few tomatoes, a living room where they can relax after a*

Homes on Piquette Street near East Grand Boulevard, 1981. *Bruce Harkness.*

hard day's work and feel secure. They should have it. They have earned it, if not on Trombly in some place like it.[126]

Many residents continued to think it was a rumor until they saw moving vans and relocation packets arrive. Others were completely surprised by the news. They gathered in the streets, asked questions, fretted. Some took it very seriously and were concerned. "One day this young woman knocks on my door and tells me my place isn't mine," Mrs. Barnett, a Poletown resident, told a reporter for *The Citizen*. "I said, 'Yes, it is, I have the deed.' Do you know what she told me? 'That deed doesn't mean anything,' she said, 'You can verify it downtown.'"[127] The residents were not against the plant. They wanted the plant and understood the importance of the plant, just not at the cost of their neighborhood, their church, their lives. But officials said the area was blighted and the few residents who lived there could be sacrificed for the good of Detroit's economy.

For a *Free Press* article titled "How Much Must Cities Give to Big Business?," citizens were able to send in their opinions of the proposed GM plant for publication. One citizen wrote on September 5, 1980:

> *When and where will urban black mail by large, multi-national corporations end? Here in Detroit, the General Motors Corp. demands from the city an area the size of downtown Detroit to build an assembly plant. Because of GM's threats to relocate outside the city limits, Detroit will lose one of the last remaining racially harmonious neighborhoods. Hard on the heels of the GM threat comes the announcement from Chicago that the Hilton Hotels Corp. has received from that city's government a virtual veto power over a six-block zone where it wishes to build a hotel. The 32-page contract demands that the city demolish many buildings that some preservationists are trying to save. Failure by the city to assemble all of the property would result in Hilton withdrawing its building plans. How much longer will city governments be forced into so-called politically justified decisions that are against the will of you and me, the struggling taxpayers?*

Another citizen, George Somaczyck, argued:

> *We should strip the proposal and see it for what it is in its most naked form. It is a vicious disregard of people for the sake of profit and power. All the rhetoric from GM about concern for Detroit is a smokescreen for its own dominating interest, increasing profit. ... When you destroy homes, churches*

The interior of Famous Bar-B-Q Restaurant on Chene Street, 1981. It was owned by Carl Fisher, whose father had come to Detroit from Greece. The restaurant served the neighborhood for over forty years before it was razed for the GM plant. *Bruce Harkness.*

and institutions to which people have been tied, you destroy the people. This is the real game that is being played and these are the stakes.[128]

The news of the project did not come without casualties either. Father Maloney told the story of one of his parishioners who came to him distraught with the city's relocation booklet in her hand. The woman left his office and, when she returned home, jumped out her apartment window to her death. Another resident who witnessed this distressing sight went into cardiac arrest and had to be hospitalized.[129]

General Motors and Coleman Young

Coleman A. Young Papers: "Note: No documents for Jan. 1979–Dec. 1980"
                        —Walter P. Reuther Library

A deal on this scale would have taken a lot of time and planning. But one might find it peculiar that the papers Coleman A. Young himself submitted to the Walter P. Reuther Library at Wayne State University are missing the exact months he and General Motors, along with the archdiocese, would have been planning the new Central Industrial Park Project (CIPP). Did he personally omit these years from his collection? If so, *why?* Proper protocol would have called for him and his staff to document meeting minutes or at the very least have some evidence that prior thought was put into this, especially when it came to why General Motors thought it was necessary to build an entirely new plant in an economic recession (an automobile recession) instead of repurposing some of its other plants (Clark Assembly and Fleetwood) rumored to shut down prior to building the CIPP. But the only evidence of discussion was the secret meeting of the council, called together by the Community and Economic Development Department's Emmett Moten on June 25, 1980. In this meeting, the city council was shown the full plans, *already drawn up and plotted out.* In addition to the omission of Young's papers for this year, what is even more disturbing is that Cardinal Dearden's calendar for 1980 has also vanished.

Coleman Young was elected during one of Detroit's worst economic crises in the city's history. In 1980, market values for the American automobile dropped when U.S. corporations were consistently outsold by the Japanese. Advertisements for GM automobiles in the late 1970s and 1980s emphasized fuel efficiency and roominess with a hint of foreign market repulsion.

The crash of the auto industry affected not only Detroit's economy but the nation's as well. In that same year, Congress gave Chrysler Corporation a bailout to remedy its $3.1 billion loss in the market, but this did not come without its employees agreeing "to make wage and benefit concessions valued at more than one billion dollars [with the UAW]."[130] The thought was that a bailout would boost the nation's economy, but the recession only became worse, and Michigan seemed to be an inadequate place for ambition, as folks moved out of the state looking for jobs elsewhere. In 1980, the unemployment rate rose to a little over 18 percent in the city, not too far from the 25 percent it had reached for the nation during the Great Depression.

Alan Ackerman, the condemnation attorney for many of the residents in Poletown, stated, "[Coleman Young] didn't go to GM, they came to him. And GM was a much different company in 1979 and 1980 than it is today. [Detroit] hadn't had any new project in the city with more than a hundred employees since 1958 or 1960. It was just so bleak at that point in time. So, it was very exciting for everyone in the city. It wasn't great for the people in the [Poletown] neighborhood—that was the old type of neighborhood where people were tied to their [community]. It was tough."[131]

Since the evidence seems to have gone missing, no one will ever know exactly how the deal was worked out, how the neighborhood known as Poletown was chosen out of the other properties Young laid out for the corporation, but we do know that certain stipulations came with the deal. GM knew it could go just about anywhere in the country and cities would "fall all over themselves" to accommodate the company, Councilman Kenneth Cockeral articulated so well in the 1983 film *Poletown Lives!*[132] So by this, Coleman Young himself was in a tight spot, and it seems he would have done just about anything to solidify the deal for his city.

Dollars and Cents

Somewhere in the heart of Washington, D.C., consumer protection activist and attorney Ralph Nader happened to be flipping through the *Washington Post* in late November 1980 when he came across a story about the auto industry and the fate of a small neighborhood in Detroit, mentioned at the very end of the article on the next page among advertisements. "No one had contacted us before this, it was a random notice, a random discovery by Mr. Nader," said Gene Stilp, who was an associate attorney for the Ralph Nader team at the time. He described the find as a "very random, accidental discovery," noting that the neighborhood's fate was not addressed until much later and only briefly in the continued portion of the article. Such would be the problem for Poletown residents; their fate would be a small matter to most who desperately needed the promised six thousand jobs.

The residents were told they would get paid for their homes and businesses (anywhere between $4,000 and $15,000) and they were also going to receive a check for any additional costs of relocation. But naturally the people had a lot of questions about the legality of their forced removal and began to organize. Reporter Louis Cook asked the questions many of the residents were asking: "What kind of a new house can one buy for $15,000? Where can you go? What kind of a price can be put on a home that is rich in memories?[133] On October 14, 1980, a meeting with the CEDD and other city officials, including historical preservation experts, was held at Kettering High School to discuss the Central Industrial Park project with residents. With more than one thousand people at the meeting, Olechowski and Hodas passed out pamphlets to get residents organized against the project. They created the Poletown Neighborhood Council

(PNC). Their first meeting was conducted in the basement of Immaculate Conception. Four hundred people attended.[134]

The PNC devoted a lot of its time attacking the environmental impact report, something that needed to be rock solid and well thought out before both Hamtramck and Detroit could get the federal funding necessary to initiate the plan. In September 1980, the City of Detroit had applied for about $130 million worth of federal grant money. Meanwhile, the project itself would cost the city an estimated $200 million, with a $70 million shortfall, while GM would invest a mere $80 million for the land.[135] Some criticized the imbalance of the investment. But if the construction work and supplies needed for the job had been factored in—these supplies and the workforce all coming from Detroit—then there were *some* financial benefits to the project, albeit brief.

In the end, GM's estimated project investment would be $500 million.[136] Coleman Young had no choice. He did everything in his power to make the deal happen. This included an illegal use of the eminent domain law, though at the time it was considered legitimate, but the real kicker, which many felt was plain inhumane, was the quick-take clause written into the law that allowed the city to take the 465 acres in only ten months. This, of course, meant that residents had to find new homes, pack up their belongings and vacate the land in less than a year and, in some cases, against their will.

The Poletown Neighborhood Council was still working on ways to penetrate the Environmental Impact Report when an attorney from Ralph Nader's Center for the Study of Responsive Law stepped out of a taxi in the middle of Poletown. Gene Stilp said it was the second of January when he first came to the area. He remembered being surprised that it was indeed a *neighborhood*. "There was at least a foot of snow on the ground. It was a cold day and while walking around the neighborhood, T.V. cameras followed me around, I felt I was in the middle of the battle." When he learned about the meetings being conducted at Immaculate Conception Church, he went there. "The next step for me was to get more activists in there and get more of Nader's writers there as soon as possible." He said at first it wasn't his job to tell people what to do to fight the project but rather just listen to them.[137] With Stilp's recommendation to take on the case, a team from Ralph Nader's office came to help, including Nader himself. Given Nader's history with the city and his denouncing the auto industry's lack of safety improvements for consumers in his book *Unsafe at Any Speed*, he wasn't exactly welcomed by the media or Mayor Young. In a particularly cruel article, Harry Cook of the *Detroit Free Press* summed up the situation in Poletown like this:

Egged on by Ralph Nader's butting skies, who came all the way from Washington, D.C. what was left of the congregation turned a big brick repository of plaster-of-Paris statues into a fake symbol for resistance against a "bad" mayor and a "greedy" corporation. The frail priest, the Rev. Joseph Karasiewicz, was shoved into the glare of klieg lights, and his sincere piety was exploited by those who should have known better. Before long the myth of Poletown was born and the church, built in 1928, was called "historic," as the Cathedral of Notre Dame in Paris is called historic. Verily, there are asphalt parking lots in Detroit that have greater vulnerability than the Immaculate Conception edifice.[138]

In this passive-aggressive and rather smug report by Cook, he echoed the very words stated by Coleman Young, who also argued on numerous occasions that the neighborhood of Poletown was a myth, that Poletown didn't exist, that it was not a real neighborhood or united community before Olechowski came up with the name. Actually, as stated earlier in this work, the name "Poletown" was given to the neighborhood by reporters in the 1880s. The name floated in obscurity for a good hundred years before Olechowski brought it back as a marketing tactic to give the neighborhood a definitive name, so when it was reported about, as it fought for its life, people would associate it with something living and breathing, as it certainly was.

The Nader group began to work on plans to reconfigure the parking lot for the GM plant and use rooftop parking instead, which would ultimately save a good chunk of the neighborhood. In the original design, the plant itself would take only a quarter of the 465 acres it wanted, with the Immaculate Conception Church and most of the neighborhood being bulldozed for a parking lot and shrubbery. This was the driving point for the fight. One reporter noted that if the "GM plant undeniably represents progress," then why is it destroying a neighborhood just to take up more land than it needs?[139] Progress has many different definitions, and some would not define the word in terms of money spent but rather the ways in which a community comes together to help one another. The reporter went on to say that his "gripe" was that "out of the 460 acres in the site, more than one hundred will be devoted to parking lots. "Imagine that," he wrote, "I had honestly thought our society had progressed beyond the point where we destroy houses people live in to create spaces for cars to sit in."[140] When the neighborhood itself seemed doomed, the church became the focus of salvation since it was the center of the resistance, and it became the symbol of the fight itself.

"You Don't Have to Be Polish to Love Poletown" bumper sticker. Poletown stickers and pins were common among the residents who were against the GM plant. *Hamtramck Public Library.*

But the media and people living outside the doomed neighborhood could not sympathize with the residents amidst the economic recession. In the media, GM was crowned a hero for coming to the city's rescue. While residents sent letters out to help spread the word about what was happening to their neighborhood, hoping others would help or send letters to their representatives, "GM consistently described the new plant as a public service," pointing to the city's use of the eminent domain law and the "quick-take" clause. The quick-take clause, which allowed the city to take the land within ten months, was essential to solidifying the deal with GM. If this clause had not been written, the condemnation of the land would have taken years. GM made its usual threat: if the city failed to take the land quickly, it would go to another state. Lee Iacocca of the Chrysler Corporation stated in an interview that this sort of thing was normal. "Ford, when I was there, General Motors, Chrysler, all over the world, we would pit Ohio versus Michigan. We'd pit Canada versus the U.S., etc."[141]

Emmett Moten stated in an article from October 1980 that one of the stipulations of the deal was that if the city did not come through with a tax abatement of 50 percent for twelve years, GM would withdraw its offer. "If we do not deliver on this, they will not build." Taxes on the new plant were expected to be about $21 million a year, Moten said. The abatement was subject to city council approval. Councilman Kenneth Cockrel, who was against the proposed plan, said, "GM is blackjacking the council by saying we have to give a tax break or go to hell. That's the bottom line."[142] In addition to this, the article states that the deal could fail if the city "is unable to raise more than $300 million in federal funds to acquire the 465 acres, relocate 3,438 residents and demolish 1,176 buildings." Articles like this promoted doubt in the fruition of the project among Poletown residents. Poletown resident John Saber believed the impoverished city wouldn't be able to afford the project and thought he'd wait it out (in the meantime, he

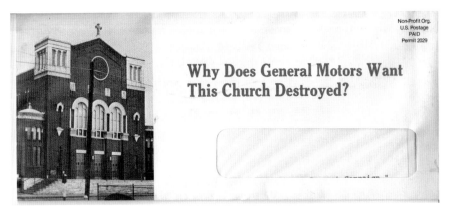

Example of a Poletown letter asking for help from surrounding Detroit residents. *Hamtramck Historical Museum.*

sued the city for their unlawful taking of his property). His standoff lasted until March 1982, when the city ordered his forced removal from his home.

Residents called the deal "corporate blackmail," and Ralph Nader called it "corporate socialism." "This is not capitalism; this is corporate socialism embodied in General Motors," he announced in a press conference shortly after his arrival to Poletown, going on to emphasize that the city wasn't simply paying the residents for their homes but instead was "subsidizing them for the privilege of making a profit."[143]

In one *New York Times* article written in the spring of '81, a reporter seemed to split his opinion rapidly. He spoke of dollars and cents in the case of Poletown. "Detroit is hurting," he wrote. "Unemployment in the Motor City is up to eighteen percent and benefits are running out. Nowhere in America is economic depression more a reality." The article goes on using the same marketing lingo General Motors had used to sway citizens to buy into the project despite its illegality. "Like a good corporate citizen, G.M. offered to stay in Detroit with a new plant rather than run to the Sun Belt and pointed to a 465-acre site with the needed transportation facilities. But the site is a living breathing neighborhood. It is called Poletown, so named because many of its residents are of Polish extraction. Its small houses, candy stores, churches, add up to what urban planners would call a community."[144]

Many of the people interviewed for this book said that the media treated the story fairly, but the continuation of this article takes a turn. This was something not seen often as reporters skated right along the edge of both opinion and politics, accommodating their liberal mayor by restraining themselves from speaking out about what they knew was an injustice. An outsider from the *New York Times*, world-class journalist William Safire, summarized the situation well, though its contortion is telling. Some reporters struggled with a clear argument on the matter because the politics involved were a bit twisted.

> *Some of the residents of the area, who owned the property they lived in, did not want to be paid off and told the city to leave. In their ornery, selfish way, and with no regard for the greatest good of the greatest number, they went to court to object to the seizure of their property. The Supreme Court of Michigan, 5 to 2, told them to get lost. "Eminent domain" enables the government to force private property owners to sell their property for "just" compensation—that's how necessary roads get built. The condemnation of property was surely for a public purpose—jobs for the unemployed, city taxes needed to pay welfare. But a dissenting judge, stewing over the quick decision, belatedly issued a long opinion that is stirring second thoughts. Justice James L. Ryan drew the distinction between a public use, such as a road, that can be used by all, and a public purpose, such as a job-creating private enterprise, and argued that this extension of the law of eminent domain "seriously jeopardized the security of all private property ownership." Justice Ryan wrote in his statement, "Eminent domain is an attribute of sovereignty. When individual citizens are forced to suffer great social dislocation to permit private corporations to construct plants where they deem it most profitable, one is left to wonder who the sovereign is."*

Safire then went on to finally make his point, arguing that this thinking was anti-capitalistic. "At a time when we are encouraging the Poles in Poland to turn toward capitalism, it is ironic to have Americans in Poletown facing expropriation of their property....I hope," he wrote finally, "some persnickety lawyer takes it to a higher court; not even the emergency facing Detroit justifies this abuse of the power of eminent domain that endangers everyone's right to own."[145]

Eminent Domain in the Case of Poletown

At Michigan's State of the Bar Address in 2008, a panel of lawyers and historical experts (Greg Kowalski, Jerry Pesick, Alan Ackerman, David Baker Lewis, Norm Ankers and Judge Paul Paruk) came together to discuss the use of eminent domain and why in 1981 it was passed and initiated in the seizing of Poletown for the General Motors Corporation. Jerry Pesick stated that the term had become so watered down over the course of one hundred years that its original intention became somewhat lost. Its original intention, he explained, was for municipal purposes for the "community at large."[146] He noted that "both state and federal courts had been making decisions that had been watering down the public use definition for decades. Traditionally public uses for purposes of public domain were just that, municipal buildings, parks, schools, uses that were available to the public at large. That started to change in the twentieth century when the courts began to approve taking to help establish the milling and railroad industry, by way of example, and by the middle of the twentieth century, however, public uses by which property could be taken by eminent domain had expanded even further."[147]

Because the economic condition at the time was so dire for Detroit, the courts ruled that the building of the plant, being that it would supply upward of six thousand jobs in an economic recession and possibly boost the economy for all, could be considered a public purpose. In an interview with Alan Ackerman, he stated, "It would never be of public use today. The term 'public use' had been broadly treated for years. But it was really something to be used for the public in the 1840s for the railroad services, so long as the rates are regulated. They can only make so much profit, and they can't discriminate. 'Public use' in Michigan is the first real well-defined standard of *public use*. But profit has to be regulated by government standards."[148] When it comes to corporate ownership, this last bit would have been impossible. The attorneys representing the Poletown Neighborhood Council in court knew eminent domain was being used illegally, but the *powers* manifested in the City of Detroit, General Motors, the archdiocese and the UAW had a strong footing in the court system, which yielded to their persuasion.

However, in 2004, the Michigan Supreme Court reversed its ruling in a similar case, *County of Wayne v. Hathcock*, proving that the people of Poletown and the Nader attorneys were right all along—the taking of Poletown for the purpose of the General Motors plant was illegal, thus making the story of Poletown that much more tragic.

In a CBS feature with Marlene Sanders, the GM project was discussed with regard to the civilian impact in an episode titled "What's Good for General Motors." Mike Duffy summarized it in an article for the *Free Press*. Pictured in the article was a smiling Coleman Young with the caption "Mayor

Young: as feisty as ever." Young told the interviewer, Marlene Sanders, that "GM didn't ask anything of us, we asked something of GM." Duffy wrote:

> *The city's use of a most menacing legal crowbar—the law of eminent domain, which allows private property to be confiscated for the public good, and in this case to benefit a mammoth private corporation—was upheld in the Michigan courts. But correspondent Sanders correctly points out that most Poletown residents were happy for the chance to sell "unsellable" homes for prices they could never have gotten on the open market....One resident, Mary Ternavsky, said her home would be lucky to sell for $5,000. Now she's getting $16,000 for the home and another $15,000 to relocate—the typical settlement.* [149]

According to residents, the faster you moved the more money you received. John Smigielski explained that the city would give a premium for anyone who moved immediately. Some residents decided to take the city to court for more money, especially business owners who argued that establishing their businesses elsewhere would be a damper on their livelihood. When asked about all the controversy and whether all the hassle of residents fighting back and lawsuits was worth it, Mayor Young said, "Absolutely—there's no such thing as a free lunch. And you don't get rain without thunder and lightning." [150]

Celebration for Hamtramck

The news of the Central Industrial Park Project was tremendously exciting for Hamtramck, a city in a panic after Lee Iacocca closed Dodge Main in 1979. "What we were facing back then, was the greatest threat this city has ever faced. We were really concerned about what was going to happen to us," said Greg Kowalski, executive director of the Hamtramck Historical Museum and the former editor of *The Citizen* (Hamtramck's local paper). The city had benefited from the tax income from the plant since its beginning, but not just benefited; Kowalski argued that the plant was its *core* income. And although Hamtramck had other factories within city limits, they, too, were connected with Dodge Main. Kowalski remarked that the city had made a mistake relying so heavily on Dodge Main as its main source of revenue. [151] "People were telling me Hamtramck needs six pallbearers and that it was dead," Hamtramck mayor Robert Kozaren told the *Detroit Free Press*.[152] "We knew we were on the road to bankruptcy," Kowalski said, noting that the city had experienced financial trouble in the past. "This is the one [the closing of Dodge Main] that really put the city on the line. What was going to happen to us," he asked rhetorically, "if we couldn't pay the bills, if we couldn't have a police and fire department? There was nothing on the horizon."

But in June 1980, hope appeared. "It was Saturday morning," Kowalski remembered. "I got a phone call from Mayor Kozaren, and he said to me, 'I got a story for you! General Motors is going to build a giant factory in Hamtramck…but you can't write the story now, you have to sit on the story.'" Kowalski said he kept the news a secret for three or four weeks. When it was finally published, *The Citizen* was the first to break what would become national news, beating out both the *Free Press* and the *Detroit News* for the story.[153]

However, at the time of GM's proposal, Hamtramck was still embroiled in the urban renewal case *Garrett v. the City of Hamtramck*, where the city was accused of displacing about 450 people (mostly black) for an infrastructure project in 1971 deemed as urban renewal. But evidence proved the city's motives to be more sinister. Federal judge Damon Keith ruled that the city had specifically targeted the area and was guilty of racial discrimination.[154]

To promote justice for those displaced by Hamtramck's urban renewal project, the city was ordered to build hundreds of residential units, an order that would take the city decades to complete. On top of this, Hamtramck was forbidden to tear down existing buildings (including Dodge Main) without court approval. So where did this leave the newly proposed Central Industrial Park Project?

Coleman Young had to step in and help Hamtramck make the deal possible. According to Greg Kowalski, Hamtramck's urban renewal barricade was softened with the help of Detroit's mayor, who held a Friday night meeting with Judge Keith to "grant an exception so they could tear down Dodge Main and any other buildings related to the project." Yet, when finished, Hamtramck would only own a portion of the plant and receive income tax benefits from only a handful of future employees. Mayor Kozaren had to strike a deal with the City of Detroit that Hamtramck would reap the benefits from the entire CIPP and not just the portion built within Hamtramck city limits. "That was a real battle," remembered Kowalski. But eventually, Coleman Young and Mayor Kozaren made an agreement that the plant would benefit both cities collectively. With all obstacles out of the way, Dodge Main was the first building to fall—thus began the end of Poletown.

Dodge Main falls. Image of boiler building. *Hamtramck Historical Museum.*

Opposite and above: Demolition of Dodge Main. Greg Kowalski was allowed access into the building during the demolition. He took these photos and commented that the silenced machinery and the abandoned hallways felt eerie. As the factory was built to last, the demolition company had to use dynamite to dismantle it. *Hamtramck Historical Museum*.

EXODUS

Because it's the house I remember best
Because lovely memories were made there
Because in my world it was near perfect
Because I felt safe and warm and loved
Because mom and dad were always present
Because Camellia and Mike shared my life
Because yellow brightened the kitchen walls
Because our canary sang so sweetly
Because the green glider on the front porch was so welcoming
Because neighbors were always available to help
Because the streets were lined with oaks and elms
Because my grade school was on the corner
Because my best friend lived on the next street
Because things never remain the same
Because the plans were made and carried out
Because politicians will get their way
Because they took away a neighborhood
Because a community disappeared
Because so many lives were disrupted
Because it never should have taken place
Because the Cadillac plant now stands there
I can never go home again.
—Patricia Siergiej-Swarthout, "Poletown"

Patricia saw a picture of her home boarded up in a photograph taken during the razing. It was this picture that brought on the idea for the poem titled "Poletown." She composed it for a class assignment in which she had to write about a time that truly affected her life.[155] The assignment was to write a poem with each line beginning with the word *because*, but it was the sharp turn in the tone of the poem toward the middle that captured the attention of her teacher and peers. They were shocked when Patricia relayed the story of Poletown to them.

John Smigielski's mother used to sweep her upstairs deck and talk to passersby on the street below. "The kids in the neighborhood would always check up on her and make sure she was all right." She was determined to stay in that house. Even when the real estate sharks showed up to offer her a price, she refused to sell the house for less than what it was worth.

Though some were more than happy to receive payment and leave Poletown (renters received $4,000 to relocate), some were completely heartbroken to leave the homes that had been in their families for perhaps

A man browses items for sale outside a Poletown home, 1981. Sign reads, "Yard Sale. GM wants us out! Help." *Bruce Harkness.*

generations. In some cases, elderly folks lived with their children or even their elderly sisters and brothers. Many worried about the logistics of the payment for their homes and businesses. And of course, they knew the harsh realities of starting their businesses elsewhere. The success rate of that adventure is known to be slim. "Unemployed Kenneth Colbert is still waiting to be reimbursed for the income he said he lost when the Boron Gas station he operated was razed to make way for the new factory," reported a *Detroit News* article from 1985.[156] Another resident, Alice Carter, said she expected the city to give her further financial assistance for the "decaying house" they relocated her to on Detroit's east side.[157] "Mrs. Carter, 72, said she recalls the day when she received a letter telling her the city had to clear her land to make way for the proposed plant....'We were given 90 days to relocate,' she said, 'and we couldn't take anything that was nailed down. We had new doors, new carpet, new paneling, a window air-conditioner and a new chandelier. After we moved, they went in and took everything they said we couldn't.' Mrs. Carter said she received $30,000 for the two-family flat she owned with her husband on Trombly."[158]

In 1985, after the assembly plant was built, the city was still dealing with lawsuits from Poletown. "The residents said the city violated their civil rights, not only moving them too quickly, but not compensating accurately and not putting into consideration the moving parts that resulted from the land grab."[159] Alice Carter complained that the taxes for her new home were double what she was paying in Poletown. "I know the city should owe me something," she told reporter Rebecca Powers. She and other residents sued the city for $10,000 each.[160]

However, some residents felt different. One woman felt safe in her new home near East Seven Mile. She paid $40,000 for it with the $29,000 she received from both the payment from the city for her house and the relocation money combined. "For 12 years my youngest daughter was like a prisoner. I had to watch her all the way down the street to her friend's house. I had to walk her back and forth to school. Where we are now, I feel safe."[161]

"Two weeks after the city approved the plan, a small troop of yellow-jacketed Century 21 real estate agents greeted the community with offers to find them new homes. They invited the community to a 'information packed' open house, complete with free refreshments and information about new housing in the Detroit area."[162] The agents decorated a corkboard with Polaroid photos of available Detroit homes, ranging from $20,000 to $50,000. "You don't get a shot like this every day, you know, with real estate being down. I felt with the economy like it was I would have a chance to make some money," one realtor told *Free Press* reporter Luther Jackson after the city had bulldozed most of the neighborhood.[163]

John Smigielski said after the news got out that the neighborhood was doomed, lawyers and real estate agents began to prowl the neighborhood, knocking on doors and catching folks doing yard work outside their homes. "You had these lawyers," he remembered, "coming in and giving incentives. A guy drove up in his Mercedes, he made propositions saying he could represent [the Smigielskis] at meetings and in court. But of course, he would get a third of everything my mom got. So," he continued, "we got the letter from the city saying this is what you're going to get if you move out at this time. My brother and I said, 'Mom, let's just get you the heck out of here—take the money and run. You're not going to get much more, all they want is the property, and they need this building.'"

About a year before GM's plan was publicized, a man approached Smigielski's mother about buying the funeral home. Smigielski said men would buy the homes and move two or three families in, then profit off the city checks and relocation packages. Smigielski said that the men buying homes from the willing probably knew something the residents didn't. The news of the project had not been publicized yet, but their buying was so prevalent, he assumed after the fact that they were after the relocation money. John and his brother tried to convince his mother to sell the funeral home to one of these prospective buyers because real estate prices for that area were so low. But Smigielski's mother refused the deal, something they were thankful for when the relocation packets arrived.

His mom bought a condo with her social security benefits. The city gave her a low-interest loan, so she was able to handle it, but she was only there for six weeks. She went to the hospital because she was malnourished and depressed. They put her in a psych ward to try to get her out of her depression, but a month later Mrs. Smigielski passed away.

The Resistance

When you're in a deep sleep, it takes a deep shock to wake you up.[164]

Deb Choly, a law student from Wayne State University, first heard about the new plant in the news, but she didn't get involved until Jeanie Wylie, her roommate and best friend, invited her to a couple meetings of the

Poletown Neighborhood Council. Wylie had been filming the story with her boyfriend at the time, George Corsetti, so she had become familiar with the residents and the attorneys working for Ralph Nader. She helped get Choly an internship that summer with the Nader attorneys. "I would hear about it from her, and during the summer I was able to get more involved. They would have community meetings at the church every week. Tom [Olechowski] was doing a lot at the beginning. George and Jeanie and Richard [Wieske (cameraman)] would show up and film different things, then in the summer of '81, all the political pieces fell into place. All the forces in Detroit lined up in favor of this plant."[165]

Choly worked with the Nader staff to come up with a different plan for the parking lot, which would have saved a great deal of the neighborhood. "When Ralph Nader got involved, they really put pressure on the forces, but it was a little late." Choly said the attorneys hired experts to redesign the GM plans. "But the political wheels had been turning, and I don't know if there was anything we could have done at that point."

Gene Stilp said they had to meet architects who worked closely with the city way out of town so no one would see them. Stilp elaborated on this, saying, "Our intention was to find a way of coexistence. So that Poletown could exist and the plant could exist, but the outside of the plant, the parking lots and the railyard had to be redesigned. So we tried to show that in court, but we needed an expert to present it because we didn't have the expertise."

The Nader attorneys had a tough time finding any railroad experts who would talk to them. The "experts" feared they would be blackballed in the industry for consorting with the resistance. "We had to meet with one guy in Flint," Stilp remembered, "undercover and at a certain time, late in the evening, to try to get pointers on how the railyard shipping could be redesigned to save the neighborhood so we could give testimony that we had an alternative."[166]

"We had all the information," said Choly when asked if there was anything more the attorneys could have done to save the neighborhood or halt or expose any shady deals going on behind government and corporate doors. "We knew what was going on. Even if there were any 'shady' things going on, the economics in Detroit had been so dire that anything the city could do to bring some jobs, people were going to support, and in fact that even influenced the Michigan Supreme Court—that it was for a public purpose—which has been debunked since."[167]

On the national level, a heated debate occurred in St. Louis, Missouri, in June 1981 when the American Council of Polish Cultural Clubs (ACPCC) passed a resolution in support of preserving the Immaculate Conception Church.

> *The Board of Directors of the* [ACPCC] *hereby protests and condemns the agreement between the General Motors Corporation and the Archdiocese of Detroit to bring about the destruction of Immaculate Conception Church, and the methods by which that agreement was reached by General Motors and Cardinal Dearden, the former Archbishop of the Archdiocese of Detroit; and the American Council of Polish Cultural Clubs demands that the Archdiocese of Detroit utilize any proceeds received from the sale or transfer of Immaculate Conception Church and any contents thereof exclusively for the support of the remaining five Polish Poletown parishes, and redress the wrong done to the Polish-American Community in Poletown, in funding the construction of a cultural center in Detroit, for the preservation of the history and culture of Polish-Americans of the region for posterity.* [168]

Richard Hodas added to this statement,

> *The fact that* [the ACPCC] *did attempt to assist us in whatever way possible indicates that other Polonia Organizations could have done the same. Those who came forward with support for Poletown deserve to be commended, they defended the rights of all owners of homes and businesses in Michigan to the security of their property. However, because of the legal mechanisms through which the GM project had been undertaken, no home, no business, no neighborhood in the state—including Hamtramck—is secure. They could be demolished against the will of the people legally by any power that has received the authorization to do so.* [169]

"My house has a new bathtub, and I don't intend to move because you con-artists want to pull a rip off," John Saber—possibly the most defiant resident in Poletown—yelled into the microphone at the first public meeting where city council members, representatives from the CEDD, an appraiser, staff people from the state and national historic preservation councils, the Citizens Districts Council and GM officials were present. Many in the audience shared Saber's opinion.

Jim Jaczkowski, a parishioner at St. Hyacinth at the time, told *Free Press* reporter Sylvia O'Neill:

> *The Polish churches are more than bricks and beams and carefully kept rituals. They are centers of the people's culture, places of personal identity. My grandparents were married* [at St. Hyacinth], *and I was baptized, made my first communion and confirmation there. You just don't see too*

many ethnic churches anymore. The artwork and everything inside there is conducive to your culture. A church is a mirror, a testimonial to your faith. If people built a church themselves with their hard-earned wages, then that is a standing prayer, a sacrifice of the people.[170]

Looters and Arson

Residents wanting to stay dealt with the inconvenience of early water and gas shutoffs. It was speculated that the city had ordered employees to shut off the utilities of homes still occupied to harass the residents and get them to move out sooner. City employees were supposed to only shut off the water and gas in houses that were clearly vacant. When they were finished, they would spray paint a large *X* on the home or business, marking it out for demolition. Unfortunately, the *X* also alerted looters and arsonists of the vacancies.

Smigielski explained: "When we left in '81, my brother and I decided we were going to take these iron baseboards we had remodeled and put on the wall that were extremely heavy. He and I decided to lift them to take these things and put them in his garage and sell them for scrap." They also planned to take a five-ton compressor they had on the air conditioner.

He and I struggled to get it up the basement to the first-floor landing. And I thought, we're nuts, we have to go get a church truck or something so we can lift it onto our trucks. And the next day we came to do it, and it was gone. Someone had busted into the funeral home and took it because they had seen us taking stuff out. They weren't too worried about getting caught or anything. Before we turned in the keys to the property, the front aluminum doors to the funeral home had been taken off, and in fact, the aluminum siding that was on the building—they had ladders—they were up there pulling that stuff off too. They were selling it all. It was disheartening.[171]

Josephine Jakubowski explained to one reporter, "Our son and his wife lived two blocks away from our place. Their home had stained glass—pink, blue and purple—and beautiful brass doorknobs. I remember they moved on a Saturday and went back on Sunday and all the glass and the doorknobs were already gone."[172]

Right: Smigielski Funeral Home in Poletown, 1981. Mrs. Smigielski lived on the second floor and was often seen sweeping her top porch. In this photo, the aluminum doors had been removed. The two Xs spray painted on the columns signaled it was ready for demolition. *Patricia Siergiej-Swarthout.*

Below: Two homes left on Adele Street surrounded by empty lots where the homes had been bulldozed and cleared away, 1981. The home on the left is occupied, while the home on the right is vacant with evidence of looting (some of the aluminum siding has been stripped). *Bruce Harkness.*

David Turnley, Pulitzer Prize–winning photographer who worked for the *Free Press* at the time, snapped a photo of two men in action, in the midst of tearing off the aluminum siding of one home. Under the photo, it explains that the two men were arrested after the photo was taken.

Wylie wrote in her book *Poletown: Community Betrayed* that police had arrested over one hundred people looting in both April and May combined. One officer reported that most of the people were from distant suburbs. And she observed that the looters acted as if they were shopping in the vacant homes.[173]

Choly said:

> As the weather broke and things got warmer, the fires started…and that was arson. That was clearly arson. And it seemed the fire department responded slowly, so things burned. Houses burned very fast. By then a lot of people left. By then a lot of people took the money from the eminent domain process and had moved, so there was a smaller and smaller group of people who were trying to fight it. They started to burn out the neighborhood. That's probably the most disturbing memory I have, to know how systematic it was. People were still living there, and there were fires going on![174]

The smoke that permeated the neighborhood night after night made it increasingly difficult for the residents who hadn't yet left. This might have been part of the strategy of the arson—to make living feel more uncomfortable and more unsafe, so anyone resisting relocation would give up their fight and evacuate. Some nights the fires were too numerous, leaving firefighters to choose which fires they would let burn and which they would quell.

"The demolition people from the city were basically in cahoots with people who take a little bit of money to start a fire," speculated Gene Stilp when asked about the arson.

> It's much easier to take down a building that is damaged by fire than one that's still standing solid. One night there were seventeen fires in Poletown among the vacant houses. They threatened the lives of people. The fire department knew it was arson and the city knew it was arson. The city benefited from it; they turned their heads the other way, and I think a lot of lives were jeopardized because of it. A lot of firefighters' lives were jeopardized.[175]

Ms. Eileen Kocieniewski

Archbishop Edmund Szoka

Dear Bishop Edmund Szoka:

About one month ago several of my frineds and I heard about the destruction
of Poletown,and Immaculate Conception Church. I am proud of my Polish heritage
and I ask you, being a Polish bishop, one of the few in this country, to make
attempts to try and save the church.

In the best interest of all Polish Americans

Eileen S. Kocieniewski

Eileen S. Kocieniewski

A letter from Eileen S. Kocieniewski to Archbishop Szoka regarding Immaculate
Conception. *Archdiocese of Detroit Archives.*

In June, the city began to crack down on vandalism and looting with signs
that read, "$100 fine to enter vacant Poletown bldgs." They also had more
police patrolling the area.[176]

John Saber, who refused to move, built a cinderblock wall around his
house, claiming that anyone who entered his property would be shot. He
threatened he would plant nothing but rose bushes in his backyard so
intruders would get "smacked in the face with thorns." He sat all day with
a shotgun on his lap, guarding his home from looters and arsonists like one
would in an apocalyptic crisis. As previously mentioned, Saber managed to
hold off the bulldozers until March 1982, when he was handcuffed and taken
out of his house. "Officers wrestled Saber to the floor while Roger Saber,

John's adult son, handed the police the .22. Saber, yelling, 'This is worse than what's happening in Warsaw,' was taken away in a squad car. A moving company filled three vans with Saber's possessions, which included reels of World War II aerial film that he had shot, a train set, and boxes of news clippings. Everything was put into storage."[177] With nowhere to go, Saber spent the rest of his days traveling from his sister's house to a Detroit bus station.[178] "By 1984 Saber was gaunt, having been hospitalized several times for malnutrition. He claimed to all who would listen that he was suffering from 'mental anguish' resulting from the GM project."[179]

As the neighborhood emptied out, the residents turned their attention to saving the Immaculate Conception Church, the established haven for the resistance and Ralph Nader's team of attorneys. Letters to the pope and the bishop were penned by passionate parishioners both past and present, people from all over the state and the nation begging his Eminence to do *something* to save the church.

The Last Moments of Poletown

In 1928, the consecration of Immaculate Conception Catholic Church was a celebrated thing. People lined the sidewalks as a marching band procession escorted Bishop Gallagher to the church. The Mass and sermon were given in Polish by Father Bortnowski, with the following message in English from Bishop Gallagher. A part of his sermon was highlighted by reporters as he announced, "Today is a day of triumph for every member of this parish. It is triumph over human selfishness, a triumph of Christ in your hearts. This unique temple stands as a monument to you."[180]

Fast-forward to 1981 and Immaculate Conception was in the news again with the headline "GM Breaks Ground in Poletown, a 'Day of Triumph,' Young Says."[181] In the course of Immaculate Conception's history, only five priests—Father Bortnowski, Father Rynazski, Father Cendrowski, Father Balazy and Father Karasiewicz—had worked to uphold the vision of Bishop Gallagher in 1928, but with a massive recession, that vision—"a triumph over human selfishness" and a "triumph of Christ" in the hearts of men—was lost.

In 1980, parishioner attendance had gone up. The number of families had increased by ten.[182] The church had a vibrant new priest and the recent sale of its school. Things were looking up. Father Karasiewicz, as most priests

Immaculate Conception parishioners pray around the grotto of Immaculate Conception for the annual May crowning of the Blessed Virgin, 1981. *Bruce Harkness.*

do when they begin life with a new parish, had hopes and dreams for the parishioners and himself at Immaculate Conception and how they might grow together. But that hope and the feeling of contentment was short-lived.

On April 30, 1981, Father Karasiewicz received a visit from Gerald Chuhran, director of archdiocesan properties, with an order not only to collect the church keys and records but also to remove Father Karasiewicz himself from the property. In a press conference, Father Karasiewicz commented that he was told by the city he could stay in the church until June 17. He knew the chancery had originally set the date for April 30 but also said it was negotiable. So it seems there was a miscommunication among Father Joe, the archdiocese and the city. Father Joe insisted that in letters from the archdiocese regarding the records there was no mention that *he* would have to leave, though a spokesperson from the archdiocese said a letter was sent to Father Karasiewicz stating that he would. Father Joe called the representatives from the chancery barbarians. "I'm not bucking any one person, I'm bucking evil, so to speak. If there is evil in the chancery then I'm bucking evil there," he stated at a "hastily called" press conference.[183] The new date for the suppression of the Immaculate Conception was then set and agreed on by all parties for May 10, and Father Joe planned to comply with the city's order to leave the church on June 17. This was after a brief legal fight by the Nader team, whom Cardinal Dearden also tried to evict from the basement of Immaculate Conception on April 30, but since Father Joe renewed their lease of ten dollars per month, which is what they had been paying since their arrival, they would carry the status of "renter" in court in the case of an eviction. Any legal measures would ultimately involve a complicated court case.[184]

In the midst of all these decisions regarding the suppression of a historic and ethnically significant church, residents were disgusted by the fact that Cardinal Dearden traveled to the suburbs around this time to bless a newly opened Gucci store. Records show that his blessing was as follows:

All about us here we see evidence of human artistry. May it lead us to You, the source of all that is beautiful. In that spirit we beg your blessing, Almighty Father, upon this enterprise, those who labor here, those whose craftsmanship is displayed here, those who will possess and enjoy these artistic creations. May we all be moved by a spirit of reverence and humility in our lives. We ask this in the name of the risen Christ, our savior, Amen.[185]

On the day before Mother's Day 1981, the residents became even more defiant when they saw that all hope was gone. They hoisted a bulldozer onto a loading truck and drove it to Roger Smith's home in the suburbs with flowers and a sign that read, "For Mrs. Smith/A Bulldozer for Roger/Save our church."[186] They presented the flowers to the guard at the gates of the chairman's suburban mansion. "This is a gift from the mothers of Poletown to Mrs. Smith. They're hoping that her Mother's Day will be as happy as it is for them, seeing their homes and churches being destroyed by Mr. Smith and his people."[187] The guard was clearly nervous, as seen in George Corsetti's film, *Poletown Lives!*, but he meekly listened to what the crowd had to say and then politely asked them to leave.

When Joe Stroud, editor of the *Free Press*, decided he would go to Sunday Mass on Mother's Day (the next day), he was struck by the experience. He wrote about it in an article for Monday's paper:

What made me go to Immaculate Conception for Sunday Mass I am not quite sure. I am not Catholic, I am not Polish, and we [the paper] *have supported the building of the new Cadillac plant as, on balance, a good thing for the city.…At the service I found myself thinking, "What if this were my church, my neighborhood?" It would hurt, and it would heal no wounds for anyone to speak of the greater good, the need to preserve jobs and rebuild the city. It would not really comfort me for someone to say the neighborhood was already near death before the process of building this plant ever started. It would not comfort me to be reminded that death is sometimes a part of renewal.…On Sunday I found myself stirred by the sobbing of Polish women near me. I found myself angered at the ravages of time and the impersonal forces of change in the city. Much of the service was in Polish, but the language of pain is universal.…The choices the politicians or the community leaders or the church hierarchy made weren't easy. I'm sure they have thought, as I have, that what had to be done had to be done. But is there no room now for the healing gesture, the compassionate response? Is there no magnanimous act that could take the curse off the process? I really don't know. I only know that on Sunday I found my heart with those who wept and prayed at Immaculate Conception.*[188]

It was Immaculate Conception's *last* Mass. Hundreds of people crammed into its sanctuary; people stood and leaned anywhere they could find a spot. Though reporters were there to witness the solemn celebration of what was an outstanding fight, though it was lost, many of them felt like Stroud. Having had to court a veil of indifference for the past few months, they could now allow themselves a moment of spiritual reflection, and this resonated in their stories. Over the course of many months, those closest to the story witnessed firsthand what it was to be powerless in America and approached the situation with humility. One reporter even went home to change her outfit because she felt severely underdressed for the church service:

Sandy Livingston was touched by Father Karasiewicz's consideration that morning. She came to take photographs and quickly realized she was going to be uncomfortable in blue jeans. When she saw Father Joe her, "heart sank. I thought he'd probably tell me to leave. Instead he offered me a chair on the side of the altar, told me to make myself comfortable and told me he had no qualms about my taking pictures. Needless to say, after about ten minutes of extreme discomfort, I went home and changed. I was struck by his consideration—especially since it was the last Mass and he must have had a great deal on his mind. Although he was very conservative, he gave no hint that my jeans were inappropriate."[189]

The sermon by Father Joe talked about the tragic fate awaiting the church. "This is not a supermarket. This is not a dance hall. This is a building dedicated to Christ and to prayer—to our blessed Lord and blessed Mother."[190]

As the church emptied out after Mass, those protesting the plant held vigil every night afterward in the basement of Immaculate Conception to protect it from looters and arsonists. The original eviction date of March 18 was moved out of courtesy for the residents to June 17. This gave the people ninety days to either leave the church or save it. "I'm no longer pastor," said Father Karasiewicz, optimistic he could save the church. "I'm a tenant of the city. The closing of the church was done only with a scrap of paper. I see no reason why it can't be changed with a piece of paper."[191]

On May 12, the day after Immaculate Conception's last Mass, Emmett Moten wrote a letter to archdiocesan director of finance Louis Woiwode about the situation at Immaculate Conception. "As you are aware," he wrote, "Father Joseph Karasiewicz and others are presently occupying the Immaculate Conception Church and the church rectory. Please be advised that the City of Detroit has not and will not accept possession and responsibility for the church until such time as it is vacated by Father Joseph Karasiewicz and the others presently occupying the church."[192]

By May 14, hope appeared when General Motors announced it was willing to move Immaculate Conception. Some say this idea stemmed from the fact that in 1954, the old Mariner's Church was moved for the Detroit Civic Center.[193] Composing a "For Immediate Release" statement to the press, the chairman of General Motors, Roger Smith, had this to say:

The plan to move the church will involve a short, but important distance. When moved, the church will be refurbished, landscaped and provided with a paved parking lot. With all of this, we believe the church will actually be in better shape physically than it is now.... We have made extensive studies of alternate plant layouts and possible rearrangements of the current site and there is just no possibility of the church remaining in its present location if we are to build a modern and efficient plant that will allow us to be competitive in the years ahead.[194]

When the news got back to Immaculate Conception that day, Father Joe came running into the sanctuary. "As rain fell in Detroit's Poletown, five women stood singing a Polish hymn in the cavernous nave of ICC, when suddenly [Father Karasiewicz] ran from the rectory into the church. He genuflected and kissed the tile floor in front of the altar. The song faded as the priest clapped his hands for attention and said: 'I just got the news. The church has been saved. Yes, it has been saved. Praise God.'"[195]

Shortly after this relocation plan was announced, Cardinal Dearden refused the offer. Those opposing the plant saw GM's ill-thought gesture as a plot by the corporation to promote good press for itself, because GM had been increasingly worried about the bad publicity it received because of Poletown and because the corporation usually made their plans official on paper before publishing press releases for proposals not approved by all parties. It was not only the residents who charged GM with this sloppy gesture—a moral slip—but it was written and reported by the media. GM was therefore accused of "pre-planning" the announcement just for some good publicity.[196]

For those looking purely at the business end, the archdiocese's dismissal of GM's plan was understandable. The city had labeled the neighborhood as *blighted*, and the archdiocese was aware of Immaculate Conception's financial history. "Immaculate Conception no longer exists as a parish," announced Mayor Young. "For years its membership has steadily declined, and on that basis, there is no sound reason for re-establishing the parish in that immediate area."[197] The people waiting for the news, good or bad, at Immaculate Conception were disappointed but even more so that they had to hear the news from a *Free Press* reporter. To the archdiocese, the few parishioners Immaculate Conception gained in the late 1970s was nothing compared to the $1.3 million the archdiocese was expected to get from the sale of the church. "For the archdiocese, the question was whether to maintain a declining church in a neighborhood that was, even before the Cadillac assembly plant was announced, losing its ethnic identity and loosening its ties with the parish."[198] The same reporter mentioned, "It will be forever an irony that, while General Motors was able to respond to the symbolism and sentiment the church had come to represent, the archdiocese was not."[199]

But it was all for show. All the announcement did was take some of the anger pointed at GM and put it instead on the archdiocese. In response to shrapnel the archdiocese received as a result, Cardinal Dearden offered to build a small side-chapel using artifacts from Immaculate Conception in a neighboring Catholic church.

"We have over 4,000 signatures from people who want the church saved," said Hodas. "Even though no parish exists here technically, there's a steady stream of phone calls from people who want to 'join the parish.'

One parishioner in Jackson has pledged a handsome weekly donation which he mails in."[200]

"We know the church can be moved and, if GM says so, it can remain where it is, but the notion of some haphazard, slapstick, putting-together of a chapel is nonsense," said Tom Olechowski. "[GM's offer] is very cruel and designed to take GM off the hook," said Gene Stilp who also told the press that a boycott of GM products in an effort to save the church and neighborhood would be announced at the company's May 22 annual meeting."[201]

On May 27, Bishop Krawczak held a meeting to discuss the future home of a chapel that would house Immaculate Conception artifacts. Father Skalski of St. Hyacinth said that he was "sensitive to Father Joe's feelings and that the timing of the meeting was wrong. 'It's like sitting in a hospital room dividing the patient's possessions before he is dead,' he said."[202] He also went on to say that he did not see a need for the chapel at that time since efforts were still being made to save the church. He clearly indicated that he did not want to discuss the matter with Father Joe present.

But Bishop Krawczak continued the meeting: "In the event such a chapel should be built, how do you as pastors feel about the proposal? Where, in your opinion, would be the most desirable place?" he asked the priests.

Father Skalski again emphasized "that it was difficult to discuss until Father Joe says it is all over." Bishop Krawczak then posed the question: "When at a given point Father Joe feels that it is all over, are you suggesting that an Immaculate Conception Cultural Center be built at St. Hyacinth's?"

At this, Father Skalski wouldn't say but simply "expressed his feeling that talking about the matter made Father Joe feel bad. He emphasized that as a friend, he would have to back Father Joe in his efforts [to save the church]."[203]

Then Father Joe stepped in and "made it known that the people are still fighting and praying. If a decision has to be made in the future, may God forbid, people of the parish should be present. The council should be here. People have been overlooked. We lost so much good will. The church puts so much emphasis on people making decisions, but it doesn't practice it."[204]

On June 17, as promised, Father Joe packed up his one little suitcase and said goodbye to the people still occupying the church. "They had cut the wire to the lights of the church, and they made Father Karasiewicz leave the rectory," Choly remembered. "He went under protest, but he did leave."[205] According to Wylie, that day Father Joe spoke to the eighty people who prayed in the sanctuary, encouraging them even though he felt the fight should end. "Karasiewicz said that a resounding victory had been won because the message of the community had been delivered to authorities who needed to hear it. He said he hoped his bond with parishioners would continue and added that he hoped no one was bitter. It had been a good fight, and everyone should feel proud."[206]

The *Free Press* that day published an article by a columnist of religious matters in Detroit, Harry Cook, that summarized the indifference felt by people looking in on the story: "Once again, and with characteristic tolerance of fools, Cardinal Dearden explained that there was no need for a building that did not have a viable congregation to use it for the greater glory of God and serve to His human children. At the time, Immaculate Conception had less than 100 parishioners some of whom came from the suburbs." Actually, records show that Immaculate Conception had close to three hundred members at the time, though no one will ever know how financially impactful the parishioners were, but annual income in the late 1970s through its demolition remained consistently above $60,000 per year. The article went on:

> *The cardinal said, as he had said all along, that the archdiocesan authorities had decided that jobs for people in a city gasping for life's breath were more important than maintaining a super-annulated building for one Sunday Mass weekly and an occasional novena. Meanwhile, the God of Catholics is still, presumably, accessible through the act of prayer. If the faithful, who mourn for the building that once echoed with their Hail Marys and Our Fathers, deem it necessary to pray inside four walls, the Archdiocese of Detroit will surely be glad to direct them to another church building. As St. Paul told the early Christians: "We have this treasure in earthen vessels." So often Christians have mistaken the vessel for the treasure.[207]*

About two weeks later, the Nader team announced it was leaving. "At that point," Deb Choly said, "everyone felt pretty abandoned, but then people moved into the church and they stayed there twenty-four hours a day. They rotated, but there were always people."[208] It had become increasingly hard for the lawyers to work because of the absence of light and the archdiocese had come and taken all the movable items by that point. According to Wylie, during their going-away gathering that night held in the church, the Parke School caught fire.

By July 2, the church was still occupied. Mats were laid out on the floor, a bathtub in the rectory was filled with water, the door was barricaded with a two-by-four and a guard was ordered to not let in any police. One reporter described the scene:

> It being mid-afternoon, most of the 15 or so individuals who nightly bed down in the lower church hall had returned home. Just one of the Nader support team members remained, the other's having left a few days before for Washington. The church with its stately façade and ornate interior could give pointers to other churches built today. It is still the salient structure of this neighborhood. But with so many of the houses near it cleared away, it now resembles a piteous giant, a shorn Samson. Inside, a lone woman kneeling in the first pew prayed....Whereas the church interior basked in veiled sunlight, the lower hall was enduring its second week of Egyptian darkness, as the old timers would say. Since June 23rd, candles and lanterns have furnished the only light. Water and prepared food are being supplied by friends of the Alamo of Poletown....A skeleton crew occupied the hall. During my visit reporters from United Press International (UPI) came there to interview Richard Hodas, vice president of the Poletown [Neighborhood] Council. The same day at 5:30 P.M., a larger press conference was scheduled to take place....The Angelus bell in the church tower is still rung regularly, although manually and with difficulty, as the symbol of determination....Around noon on Wednesday, Immaculate Conception was a hotbed of anxiety and confusion. Both sides of Trombly and Moran Avenues were lined with cars, some of them with hitched trailers and pickup trucks. On the shoulders of volunteer help, boxes, cartons and furniture poured from the exits of the rectory and lower church hall into the awaiting vehicles. A sense of urgent evacuation reigned. Inside the hall a loyal core of IC parishioners and supporters, about 100 people mostly of retirement age, wept and hugged one another. It could be compared with the sensation family members experience during the most difficult moment of a funeral, the final closing of the casket on the remains of a loved one... Despite the hustle and bustle in the hall, several members of the parish core vocalized their feelings. Mary Woroski began by reading a letter from a relative in Poland. The relative described a similar incident, which occurred near the port city of Gdynia, in which a government planned to demolish a church in order to build a factory. "The people there fought for the church and won. And they were dealing with the Communists, too! They were shocked to hear we're losing our church."...Ann Dolence, one of the most

active members of [Immaculate Conception,] *expressed what many of the core were experiencing. "We just can't come to grips with the thought that our church will be reduced to a mountain of rubbish," she remarked sadly shaking her head, "and after all these years of work and sacrifice. Do you think it's going to be easy to adjust?"*[209]

"We got a generator in there, and we got some water hooked up," Choly noted. "They managed it so you could stay there." Choly explained that she had just been there all day and was tired. She looked forward to going home to rest a bit before her next "shift," but no sooner had she arrived home than Jeanie called to summon her back. "Deb," Jeanie said on the other line, "you better get down here, because someone just knocked on the door. You might want to come back. The police are coming tonight." It was July 14. The residents had been occupying the church for nearly three months. There had been a lot of press about the sit-in protest in the papers, which caused the residents to think that might have prompted the city to move in on the church just then. Choly's main goal was to get as much media attention on the situation as possible. "I started calling the media trying to get people there. Because I was trying to make as big a deal of this as I could." She mentioned she was glad Taro Yamasaki, a Pulitzer Prize–winning photographer who at the time was a *Free Press* photographer, was there capturing photos in the basement. George Corsetti was there too to take footage for his film, but cameraman Richard Wiske could not make it before the police barricade. All Corsetti had was a voice recorder, which he later paired with Yamasaki's photos so the event would be captured for the film *Poletown Lives!*

"I kept holding off the police," Choly remembered. The police had repeatedly knocked on the door all night, but she held them off as she waited for the media to show up. "But fortunately, Taro [Yamasaki] was there, and he took a zillion photographs." Choly remembered that last morning vividly: "It was chilly [in the church]; people were praying in the sanctuary." The bells of Immaculate Conception rang out one last time as a call for help as the police wrapped a barricade fence around the property and a SWAT car rolled up among police vans. The bells of St. Hyacinth echoed their call to alert their own parishioners of what was going on. People gathered in the streets to witness the police rip the door off the basement side entrance with chains and a tow truck. The team of police entered quickly, racing down the steps and into the basement. "The women were freaking out, they were screaming and crying. Then the police guy kept talking to me, and I kept telling him I wasn't getting arrested. 'We don't want to arrest anybody,' he said." Deb Choly remembered that the police made it very clear that they didn't want to make arrests, but when no one would leave the church, they had to drag people out. Josephine Jakubowski, for one, yelled in protest as she entered a police van just as Yamasaki snapped a photo. This photo seems to be what most use when they sum up the Poletown story: "a bunch of grey-haired older women fighting for their church." "The sorry spectacle of 70-year old ladies being carted off in a police van made Detroit the laughingstock of the nation—just what Nader's meddlers had in mind,"[210] reporter Harry Cook wrote. But the story was much more involved than that, and their fight surely deserved more dignity. When the women learned they were being released from jail but the men were being held, the women insisted they wanted to be treated like the men. They performed a sit-in protest at the station until the police released the men too, "dropping all charges."[211]

Meanwhile, the demolition crew wasted no time dismantling the church. Spectators watched in horror as the crew wrapped a rope around the cross of the church and, after chiseling it off its post, lowered it upside down to the ground. Father Karasiewicz returned and, despite his order from the archdiocese to not speak to the press, could not resist the urge. "These people responsible for this are worse than the Communists in Poland. That is the message I gave them before, and I guess they couldn't understand it before. They might as well get it straight now." A reporter then asked, 'Even the archdiocese, Father?' 'Absolutely!' was Father Joe's answer, '...it is a criminal act. To go down to the very basic definition of stealing, it is simply taking someone else's property against their will. That's all it is. So, this property was taken away from them, the people, against their will."[212]

He then prayed the rosary with his former parishioners on the sidewalk amidst two hundred spectators of the demolition. Gene Stilp, who had recently flown in, spent the night outside Immaculate Conception. "At dawn, demolition resumed under the protection of sixty police officers." One man knelt in front of the approaching bulldozer as it worked its way toward the church. Others followed suit, and when the bulldozer changed directions the people followed. As demolition continued and the wrecking crew tore into the upper part of the rectory, Stilp managed to slip under the fence to run back into the church to force a delay. When asked why he did this, Stilp said, "The idea was to stop or delay the demolition. My intent was to hide in the church so no one could find me. The intent was to

Workers quickly dismantle Immaculate Conception after the SWAT team arrested and evicted sit-in protestors in the basement of the church, 1981. *Bruce Harkness.*

stay there as long as possible."[213] He was found in a closet and taken out by police. He was charged with illegal entry but released after midnight. His charges were eventually dropped.[214]

After the Immaculate Conception was demolished and its form merely rubble, spectators and Poletown supporters Jeanie Wylie and Deb Choly were talking on the sidewalk near the site.

> *We were wondering what we could do, what we could do that's symbolic that shows what people have gone through. And somebody said, we should just smash up a car in front of General Motors. Then a friend of ours stepped forward, and she said, "We can give you a car." So we did it. We planned it for four o'clock in the afternoon, because it's a good media time. It was just as the five o'clock shows were coming up, so the protest would be live, and Grand Boulevard would be more crowded, because it was just the start of rush hour. And that's what happened. We did get a lot of local media. The car was actually drivable, but we got a truck to tow it and*

sort of stall out right there in front of the building. And people just started
smashing it and had painted messages on it during the day.[215]

Parishioners and Poletown supporters alike used crowbars and mallets to smash up the 1964 Oldsmobile in what the news called a "counter demolition" in front of General Motors, chanting "Rip 'em up, tear' em up, boycott GM." According to a *Detroit News* article, the demonstration attracted onlookers from the streets as well as Detroit police and GM employees.[216]

"That was very cathartic for people, I think," added Choly. "It was pretty cool. I don't remember feeling tired at all because it was so amazing. And it really feels to me that that was the end." But she remembered that when Father Karasiewicz died, "that was just horrible. He was heartbroken. It was really hard for people when he died." Choly was unable to go to the funeral because she had finals that week. "That was *the* end for many people."[217]

Farewell, Father Joe

The death of Father Joe was another heartbreaking and shocking loss for many Poletown residents. On December 14, 1981, just five months after the Immaculate Conception fell, Father Joe was found unresponsive in the little room he was given at St. Hyacinth. This was an event that Deb Choly said marked *the end* of Poletown for most people.

The "iron priest of Poletown," Father Joseph Karasiewicz was born on April 29, 1922, in Detroit. He had two brothers, John and Tony, and a sister, Anne. His mother died in 1935 when he was twelve years old. His grandmother Ludwika Kotowska helped raise him. He attended St. Hyacinth and St. Ladislaus grade schools. Father Joe then went on to St. Ladislaus High School and St. Mary's Seminary in Norwood, Ohio. He was ordained on October 26, 1946.

He had a little black dog that he loved very much, and he was known to be gentle, kind and true. When he was forced out of Immaculate Conception, he was offered to live in the rectory of St. Hyacinth by Father Skalski, and it was there that he died. At his funeral, the following prayer was read: "Lord, remember your church throughout the world, make us grow in love, together with our Pope, our bishop, and all clergy." Before taking his body to its final resting place at Mount Olivet Cemetery, the funeral procession made its way past the spot marked with a small cross where the Immaculate Conception Church once stood.

Though the archdiocese may deny it, one could scope from looking at the fate of Father Joe after his eviction from Immaculate Conception that he had been somewhat ostracized from the Catholic Church. He was troubled by the fact that as the Christmas season neared, the archdiocese had yet to find him a permanent position. This could be because of his public disagreements with the archdiocese regarding Poletown.

It is rumored that he fell asleep with a book open on his desk with the line "my hour has come" underlined.[218] Most speculated that Father Joe, like some of the other older residents of Poletown, died of a broken heart.

Wishing you God's blessings, I remain

Respectfully yours in Christ,

Joseph Karasiewicz

Archdiocese of Detroit Archives.

REMNANTS OF DETROIT'S LOST POLETOWN

On the Film *Poletown Lives!*

For the year Poletown residents fought the City of Detroit, the UAW, the Catholic Archdiocese and General Motors, George Corsetti, Richard Wieske and Jeanie Wylie captured the fight from behind a camera. The goal of the film, produced by Information Factory in 1983, was to capture the story of the residents as they fought these grand powers. What would they have done differently if they had the chance? What did they do well? These were the focus questions of the film. Carol Dockery, a Poletown resident, mentioned she thought they could have started aggressively fighting a lot sooner and that could have helped some.

In 1983, the film won a blue ribbon from the American Film Festival and four other national film festival awards. Wylie discussed the film in her book as "colorful and dramatic." She highlights the fact that the film differed from other stories featuring Poletown because the focus remained on the complex situation of the residents.

In an interview with *Detroit News* reporter George Bullard, Corsetti mentioned that the film started out with a different point entirely but morphed into a story about the residents. "We started out to do a film on reindustrialization, and Poletown was to be just one example of what was happening, but we realized it was a story in itself. What those people went through is important, and the story should be preserved and passed on to other people. We tried to capture the transformation people go through as they confront the system."[219]

"There was a lot of pain in Poletown," Wylie added. "The people lost the things that meant home to them." The film "doesn't extend much sympathy for General Motors, the union, the city or the Archdiocese of Detroit, all of which come off as an unholy alliance that cost a lot of people their homes in order to make way for an auto plant."[220]

In a more recent interview, George Corsetti mentioned that the concept of saving Immaculate Conception seemed to him like an afterthought—if the community couldn't save the neighborhood, they would at least save the church. This is understandable if we look at the mentality of the residents and their culture, the ethos that the church is the center and an essential part of Polish culture. Gene Stilp said that this is a fair argument, that the church became more of a symbol of the injustices done to the people as the situation became more dire. They couldn't save the whole 465-acre neighborhood or even a portion of it, so they focused their energies on saving the church.[221]

The Scholarly Book
Poletown: Community Betrayed

Because Jeanie Wylie was there when the church came down and had frequented meetings with both the city and the Poletown residents, her book feels like a witness. She keeps the community together throughout the pages of her work even though they were being separated. She does this so well that at the end of the book when all the residents reunited for Father Joe's thirtieth anniversary celebration party of his ordination in the fall of 1981 (funded by the Friends of Father Joe Association), it feels as if the reader is united with old friends.

It was Ralph Nader who suggested someone write a book on the political paradox that was Poletown. Jeanie Wylie, a graduate of both the University of Michigan and Columbia University's journalism school, was trusted with the task. The book was published by the University of Illinois in 1989. The information it contains on the politics, the neighborhood and the economics involved is immense. It is loaded with detailed information that can be used as a legitimate citing source for all Poletown history. One could guess it has been used countless times by law students and novices alike for various projects.

Deb Choly, a law student at Wayne State University and Wylie's roommate at the time, mentioned that Wylie "was really smart. Jeanie was really *quick*—she learned things quickly. She had a great deal of agency." It was this agency that would help her produce one of the most thorough pieces of work for the memory of the neighborhood and its fight. Wylie's parents were both inspirations to her in many ways; her father was an Episcopal priest who went on to become a bishop of the Episcopal Church in a northern Michigan diocese, and her mother was the child of missionaries and grew up in China. "She [Jeanie] knew people in power her whole life." The influence of those around her gave Wylie the confidence to accomplish amazing things. "We lived in Corktown at the time. Her mother supported her while she worked on the book. That was the way her mother supported her—I mean *believed* in the work she was doing."

Choly remembered Wylie committed much of her time to the book. "She worked on it for at least a year. She was being very thorough and persistent. She would work really hard to prove her narrative, but she would never bend the narrative to serve her purpose."

In Wylie's book *Poletown: Community Betrayed*, she was merely telling the story how she saw it through firsthand experience or stories she heard from residents, newspapers and lawyers. She was right there as the story played out, so she saw a lot of it with her own eyes. It is rare to have a scholarly work written by a person who witnessed the story. Another great aspect of both the book and the film *Poletown Lives!* was that because she worked on that too, both mediums complement each other, meaning many of the same people are featured in both, so one can witness for themselves the real people who fought and their personalities play out in different ways. This gives the interested observer a really unique and well-rounded view of the event. But at the heart of her, Wylie was a justice-seeking activist. Poletown was her first arrest among others she would receive for her peaceful way of fighting against injustice—especially in Detroit and Michigan. In the case of Poletown, like most she was arrested for not leaving the basement when the SWAT team showed up. Jeanie died in 2005 from brain cancer, leaving behind two daughters and her husband, Bill Wylie-Kellermann.

The Bruce Harkness Photos

Bruce Harkness grew up in Brighton and moved to Detroit when he began school at the Center for Creative Studies. In the 1970s and early 1980s, he photographed a lot of the Cass Corridor and then went on to Wayne State to get his master of fine arts in photography. It was around then that he first heard about GM's plan for Poletown.

"I had heard of Poletown, what was going on over there, but I didn't really latch on to it, and I didn't think it was something I wanted to photograph." It was his friend Nick Valenti, also a student at Wayne, who approached him and suggested the two capture the neighborhood before it was bulldozed. "He came to me and said, 'Look, they're going to tear down this entire community. You and I should go over there and start photographing.'"[222] Nick had the idea that he and Harkness could pool their photos and make a book. Harkness agreed because his schedule was somewhat free at the time. So they drove over one day and began taking photos. "That's when it caught on with me," he said.

Valenti left the project shortly after they began, but Harkness was drawn to Poletown and felt the project was necessary for people in the future, like researchers who might need the photos. In the course of ten months—from February to late November 1981—Harkness took over five hundred photos documenting the neighborhood as General Motors closed in.

Bruce Harkness, early 1980s, exhibiting his Poletown photography. *Bruce Harkness.*

Bruce Harkness taking pictures of Poletown from the top of the Graylawn apartment building on the corner of East Grand Boulevard and Chene Street, 1981. *Bruce Harkness.*

"I liked it. One reason was because in February of '81 it was mild. It snowed just a few times in February and March." Harkness said he enjoyed the project mostly because of the atmosphere the weather had produced that season. "There was this sort of warm and misty atmosphere, and I felt safe there…and visually it was very interesting to me."

Harkness began going to the neighborhood two or three times a week. Sometimes he used a handheld camera, but most of his photos were done with a 4x5 press camera—the kind with a tripod and a dark cloth that goes over the photographer's head. "I would take eight or ten sheets of film, park in a certain area, wander around. Whatever caught my eye I would photograph." Harkness chose the large format camera to capture the detail in each photo because it was more of a documentary project. He said he would wander around and sometimes he was there for three hours and sometimes only a half hour, depending on how quickly he went through his film. "I would try to cover different aspects of [the neighborhood]," he said, "choosing one day to cover one section and another day to cover a different section." To his luck, the weather remained mild throughout the rest of winter and into spring. He said when most of the houses were gone and few people remained, he didn't go as often.

Harkness explains he was never emotionally attached to the story, but he did feel bad for those who were upset by what was happening to their homes and businesses. He spoke of Ed Niedbala, who invited him into his home, an upstairs apartment above his little liquor shop called the Chene-Trombly Market, where Ed and his wife had sold handmade kielbasa and lottery tickets since 1947. Like Father Karasiewicz, Ed had a heart attack soon after relocating out of the neighborhood. "I was an observer, a neutral recorder. I was a photographer. I just wanted to take pictures of the way [the neighborhood] looked." The trees growing on the 465 acres to be leveled also caught his interest. "I looked at the trees. The leaves had come out and they had gone through their cycle of life for decades. These trees didn't know what was going on. But I knew. I knew that this was the last time for their cycle....The cycle was going to end. These leaves were not going to come out again. But the trees stood there in their dignity....It's like knowing a person who you know is going to die—you see it differently. You treat it differently. You notice things you might not ordinarily notice."

Harkness did not know the area before coming into Poletown, so he tried to capture as much of the neighborhood as he could. "Photographers... writers, they point out something that is significant and important. But it may be in relation...more about them. *They* decide it's important. Sometimes you look at something and think that it's not compelling, but I force myself to point the camera and take the picture." Harkness does not consider himself an artistic photographer but more of a raw photographer who loves the grit of street photography. He said his photos are very straightforward. "When I was photographing things in Poletown, there were things that I thought were beautiful, that caught my eye. But then there were other things that were very mundane. I tried to be honest about photographing those things too. I didn't just want to show only the special things in Poletown. I wanted to show the ordinary for people who want to know what was really there."

Around late November or early December 1981, Harkness set off to take more photographs of the now nearly empty neighborhood. "I took my usual route, down Milwaukee [Street], and when I arrived, there was a fence. There was an eight-foot fence encircling Poletown. So I said, 'That's it, I'm done.' I got in my car and drove away. It was no longer an accessible neighborhood; it had become General Motors private property."

Pieces of Immaculate Conception

Like the residents of Poletown, pieces of Immaculate Conception were scattered all over Michigan. The bells, the altar, the icons, all the "movable" objects were sold or donated to other parishes in the diocese, but the items deemed "non-movable" became "property of the city." Any time a Catholic church is closed, the archdiocese does its best to find homes for all the artifacts in other churches. In the case of Immaculate Conception, there are three churches we know of in Michigan holding pieces of this famous historic church.

The grandest collection is the side altar at St. Hyacinth Catholic Church in Poletown East, which holds the Immaculata statue and some pieces of the altar. Records indicate that the statue was carved by Paul Landowski around 1930. Landowski was also the artist who created *Christ the Redeemer* in Rio de Janeiro. The side altar at St. Hyacinth is set up with the Immaculata and the two angels on either side of her, just how they were behind the altar in their original place at Immaculate Conception. At Immaculate Conception the angels faced the congregation, but in St. Hyacinth they face the Immaculata statue. They sit behind pieces of the original altar, and St. Hyacinth provides kneeling cushions and a place for prayer candles. The church also has the statue of the Blessed Mother from the grotto of Immaculate Conception. She sits just outside the side entrance of the church. Jim Jaczkowski said he and some others from St. Hyacinth had to repair it because it was broken by vandals at one point.

Pieces of the altar can also be found in a small parish six miles away from Petoskey, Michigan. The parish at Solanus Mission Church in Bay Shore was beyond disappointed to receive part of the altar and tabernacle from Immaculate Conception broken upon arrival. It was donated to the church by a past parishioner. Its repairs, they said, would cost $64,000 because it was an antique and made of Italian marble—basically irreplaceable.

The bells from Immaculate Conception can be found at St. Margaret of Scotland in St. Clair Shores, Michigan. There was some debate whether the church would take them in '81, but they are there today, alive and ringing a call to prayer as they did in Poletown throughout most of the twentieth century. All three bells were installed in a tower-like structure just outside the front entrance of the church. They still ring every day at noon. According to church records, the bells were "solemnly blessed in 1938." In the Catholic faith, it is said the blessing of a bell is the "same as the blessing of a child." Each of the bells from Immaculate Conception

The former bells of Immaculate Conception, St. John, St. Joseph and St. Sigmunt, still ring at noon every day at St. Margaret of Scotland in St. Clair Shores, Michigan. *Author's photo.*

was given a name upon its blessing because bells are considered the "echo of the voice of God." The bell is given the name of a saint and taken under that saint's care.[223] In the case of these bells, they were given the names St. John, St. Joseph and St. Sigmunt. In addition to being blessed, they were washed with holy water and anointed with oil. When they were transferred to St. Margaret Parish after Immaculate Conception fell, they were blessed once more in a similar ceremony.

When Immaculate Conception was in its dismantling phase, Jim Jaczkowski took pieces of brick and some pieces of the altar to build a small shrine to Immaculate Conception in his backyard in Roseville. "Using brick, stone, slate, wood and shrubbery salvaged from the church, he built a shrine to the Virgin Mary, a small place of prayer similar to a grotto that had been on the grounds of the church on Detroit's north side. It is the work of a man who believes that the parishioners deserved to have something of the church left standing."[224]

EPILOGUE

I think this is General Motor's way of saying you peasants be damned, you have no right to even say anything about anything, and we're going to show you that by making sure your church is in a parking lot, by making sure that maybe it's even on lawn and shrubbery, etc. That it's wholly unnecessary that we tear it down, but we're going to do it anyway, so you peasants will learn don't confront corporate power.[225]
—*Tom Olechowski, July 1981*

The City of Detroit was about $80 million over budget for the land acquisition of Poletown.[226] There were numerous lawsuits in which the city was entangled years later. Charles Mistele, for one, lost his coal business and sued. Because he could not use his Poletown property as collateral, he was unable to rebuild it elsewhere. Mistele's business was among 208 in Poletown, but his business had been operating since 1895. "The company employed 70 people and grossed $10 million a year through its coal, industrial vacuuming and lawn services."[227] Kenneth Colbert did not own the gas station he operated in the neighborhood but claimed he increased its revenue, and with the taking of Poletown, his livelihood was unlawfully stolen from him. Other residents complained that the housing to which they were relocated was inadequate. "James Shively filed for 110 homeowners in April 1985, he said, 'It became quite evident that there was no intention… to follow the necessary rules to make sure that the citizens were protected and getting housing that was adequate.' Federal regulations required that the government ensure that people relocated in 'decent, safe and sanitary' housing with comparable amount of space, in an 'area not less desirable,' and accessible to their place of employment."[228]

Meanwhile, the Chene-Ferry Market, built in 1920 and home to 106 different vendors, suffered the effects of Poletown's demolition. An article from the *Detroit News* highlights the dying market after the community had been dispersed. The Chene-Ferry Market just a year later said it was barely holding on after the removal of four thousand residents. "Local supporters, faithful vendors and residents of streets that escaped the wrecking ball say they are all that's left of a historic, once-bustling marketplace.…Fewer than 50 shoppers roam its hallways Wednesdays and Saturdays.…Most [vendors] admitted they began to lose money when Poletown died."[229]

In addition to Father Joe, other older residents passed away. "I was exiled from Poletown. They destroyed our roots, our home, everything. It's like taking a sixty-year-old tree and transplanting it," Walter Jakubowski told a *Detroit News* reporter.[230] Ann Giannini commented in her new home in Warren, "Something goes out of you when you put so much effort into one home and they come and tear it down. If we were forced to move, why weren't we able to go together? They had all that empty land in Hamtramck. Why couldn't they put up homes for people who want to stick together? … We don't have any new friends yet. The people are nice, but it takes a long time to be able to talk and visit like we did. Nobody sits out on their porches. I ask my husband, 'where is everybody?' He says they're watching TV. Who can watch that much TV?"[231] That was the problem for most residents not happy with their new arrangements. Much of the time, it led to depression and illness in the elderly. "George Crosby [for example] never adapted. He became disoriented and repeatedly asked to be taken home. Finally, after he had wandered away from home for three hours in bitter winter weather, he was put into a nursing home, where he died shortly thereafter."[232]

Mattie Bailey told *Free Press* reporter Vilandria King in an article titled "They Still Yearn for Poletown" that the move killed her husband. "He died with a broken heart. He knew our house. It was old but it was no trouble.…He was always running to get the [new] house fixed up, it was too much. He was my all in all. It's just me and the Lord now."[233] The Reverend Victor Nelson shared some incite about having to leave his church, the Temple of Faith Missionary Baptist Church, after five years. "I didn't want to move but I think the plant will benefit the city and give more people work. I hated to lose church members, but the community was deteriorating fast…It's hard to lose friends; it's a strain on the mind.

You never can replace what you lost."[234] In addition, the Feagans reopened their lawn mower repair shop on the east side but commented that it took them years to get consistent clientele. "This eminent domain," said Ethel Feagan, "they can take it and shove it. If they can take my business from me, honey, they can do it to anybody."[235]

The GM Detroit/Hamtramck assembly plant was in test production by August 1985, two years behind its original opening date, which caused more resentment from former residents who argued they could have stayed in their homes longer. John Richards, an attorney with Ralph Nader's office, said the protests to save the neighborhood were justified. "GM was moving too quickly," he said, and argued that the plant could have been redesigned to save the neighborhood.[236] According to a *Detroit News* article from 1985, the plant property took up 365 acres instead of the 465 acres it said it originally needed, and it used only 177 acres for the plant itself. GM argued it needed the empty space for possible expansion. Add to this the fact that some of the unutilized land within the plant property, the railroad marshaling yard that GM said was essential to plant operations, which the Nader folks tried so hard to reevaluate for the sake of the neighborhood, went unused. GM also reported that the plant plans changed more than once and that it "started out as something old and evolved into something new."[237] One reporter who got a tour of the new plant once it opened couldn't help his feeling of remorse walking through it. He stated that it would have been nice if little memorial plaques had been built into the floor pointing out where different locations of buildings and streets once stood in Poletown so that the neighborhood would always be remembered.

The past few years have brought uncertainty about the future of the Detroit/Hamtramck assembly plant. General Motors has repeatedly changed its plans for it. Reports of its possible closing have circulated, and lately it's been announced that the plant will instead be refurbished to make electric cars. This is not unlike other conflicting reports concerning plant closings and refurbishments in the past. One employee of the Fleetwood plant commented in 1985 that they had been closing Fleetwood ever since he started working there (in 1955).

When news broke in the fall of 2018 that the plant was closing, workers were furious. They were told a little before Thanksgiving that there would be massive layoffs. According to a *Free Press* article, 814 workers were going to be laid off and relocated to a different plant while GM "retooled" the Detroit/Hamtramck assembly plant starting on February 28, 2020. General Motors reported it would invest over $2.2 million into the plant, and when finished, it would employ over two thousand employees.[238] The question, though, is can these numbers really be trusted? Questions about whether the GM plant will stay open or what it may be converted to over the past couple years have caused the story of Poletown to resurface on the front page of the papers.

It has begged the question decades later: *was it worth it?* In 1980 and 1981, GM initially announced the new Poletown plant would provide six thousand jobs. But it only provided half that, a prediction Ralph Nader astutely made when it was reported the plant would be highly automated. But the most terrible twist of the whole thing was the Michigan Supreme Court ruling that the use of eminent domain was unlawful in the case of Poletown. This means, of course, it should never have happened.

Remorseful tones in the media became audible in the final days of Immaculate Conception as reporters and everyone watching at home, instead of resenting the protestors, became instead in awe of them. The residents did not quit. They held fast to the fight and never let go. Even as their church fell, even as their homes were bulldozed, they kept up the stamina by pulverizing an Oldsmobile outside GM headquarters hours after Immaculate Conception was converted to rubble. They knew they had lost. They knew. But they continued onward, if only to inspire those watching at home. "This is my first time getting involved so deeply in something. I was too busy raising six children. Didn't seem like there was time. But there is time when you care about something," said Bernice Kaczanski. She added that after Poletown, she sympathized when she saw protestors on TV fighting for other things around the country, as she remembered when she was fighting too.[239]

Don't give up the fight for justice, Poletown residents seemed to say. With every shake of a barricade fence, with every flower they wove through its links as it blocked them from entering their beloved church, with every blow of a crowbar on the '64 Oldsmobile, they displayed their defiance.

They have left that as their legacy. They should have a statue, a memorial to their protest. Enough time has passed. Perhaps General Motors, the City of Detroit, the UAW and the archdiocese would come together and even offer to pay for it as an apology. (*Wishful thinking.*) I think the skies of justice for Poletown would smile on Detroit then.

NOTES

Introduction

1. Arthur M. Woodford and Frank B. Woodford, *All Our Yesterdays: A Brief History of Detroit* (Detroit: Wayne State University Press, 1969), 26.
2. Ibid., 38–39.
3. Ibid.
4. Gayle Thornbrough, *Outpost on the Wabash 1787–1791* (Indiana: Indiana Historical Society Publications, 1957), vol. 19, pp. 19, 20.
5. Ibid., 19.

The Lost Neighborhood

6. "Industrial Detroit: 1860–1900," Detroit Historical Society, detroithistorical.org/learn/timeline-detroit/industrial-detroit-1860-1900.
7. Ibid.
8. Ibid.
9. Allan R. Treppa, St. Albertus, "Everyone Welcome!" *Sunday Mass Bulletin*, September 28, 1980, Catholic Archdiocese of Detroit.
10. Greg Kowalski, interview, March 6, 2020.
11. Jeanie Wylie, *Poletown: Community Betrayed* (Urbana: University of Illinois Press, 1989), 2.
12. Jim Jaczkowski, interview, November 25, 2019.
13. Leslie Tentler, *Seasons of Grace* (Detroit: Wayne State University Press, 1990), 25.
14. Camille Einoder, "Polish Nation Libel," email correspondence, August 5, 2002. Bentley Historical Library.

15. "Polish-Americans Picket," *Detroit Free Press*, November 17, 1970, Dom Binkowski Collection Box 3, Polish American File, Special Events, Bentley Historical Library.
16. Thomas S. Gladsky, "Halicki Travel Agency (About)," *Polish American Historical Association Newsletter* 57. nos. 1, 2 (March 2000), polishamericanstudies.org/files/public/2000-1-Spring.pdf.
17. Tentler, *Seasons of Grace*, 30.
18. "Social and Ethnic History Report," Environmental Impact Statement: William Kessler Architects, 1980, Walter P. Reuther Historical Library, 12.
19. John Smigielski, interview, September 24, 2019.
20. Ibid.
21. Jim Jaczkowski, interview, November 25, 2019.
22. Ibid.
23. Ibid.
24. Patricia Siergiej-Swarthout, interview, October 8, 2019.
25. Jaczkowski, interview.
26. Smigielski, interview.

Neighborhood Landmarks

27. "Industrial Detroit: 1860–1900," Detroit Historical Society, detroithistorical.org/learn/timeline-detroit/industrial-detroit-1860-1900.
28. Ibid.
29. "10,000 Men Seek to Share Ford Millions," *United Press*, January 6, 1914, Henry Ford Historical Collection, www.thehenryford.org/collections-and-research/digital-collections/artifact/74195/#slide=gs-200785.
30. Richard L. Fortall, "United States Census Bureau," March 27, 1995, Michigan Population of Counties by Decennial Census, www.census.gov/population/www/censusdata/cencounts/files/mi190090.txt.
31. "Social and Ethnic History Report," Environmental Impact Statement: William Kessler Architects, Box 3, File 2–3, 12.
32. Douglas Ilka, "The Main: Historic Plant Lives On in Detroit Lore," *Detroit News*, August 11, 1985, Hamtramck Public Library.
33. Patricia Montemurri and Jocelyne Zablit, "Hamtramck Rallies after Tough Times," *Detroit Free Press*, March 24, 1987, Hamtramck Public Library.
34. Bruce Garwood, interview, March 20, 2020.
35. "The Early History of St. Joseph's Hospital," *League of Catholic Women: Bulletin*, April 1925, Catholic Archdiocese of Detroit.
36. Ibid.
37. Ibid.
38. Ibid.
39. "Home for Nurses to Be Dedicated," September 19, 1931, courtesy of the Burton Historical Library.

40. Ibid.

41. "St. Joseph's Hospital Leaves Poletown," *The Citizen*, July 8, 1981, Hamtramck Public Library.

42. Milton Marwil, "The True Story of the Cemetery in the General Motors Parking Lot!" *Jewish Historical Society of Michigan* 33 (Winter 1992), courtesy of the Beth Olem Cemetery.

43. Ibid.

44. Ibid.

45. Ibid.

46. Ibid.

47. Larry Geromin, interview, September 20, 2019.

48. "Hervey C. Parke School," Library of Congress, www.loc.gov/item/mi0160.

49. "Social and Ethnic History Report," Environmental Impact Statement: William Kessler Architects, Box 3, File 2–3, 12.

50. "Letter from Father Bortnowski to His Excellency, The Rt. Rev. Bishop M.J. Gallagher," January 3, 1932, Immaculate Conception Correspondence Letters, Folder 4, N.D., 1919, Catholic Archdiocese of Detroit.

51. "Letter from Bishop of Detroit to Father Bortnowski," August 25, 1919, Immaculate Conception Correspondence, Box 1, Folder 4, Catholic Archdiocese of Detroit.

52. "Application for Permission to Build, Make Repairs, Purchase Property, or Borrow Money," December 23, 1927, Immaculate Conception Correspondence, N.D. File 4, Archives of the Catholic Archdiocese of Detroit.

53. "Letter from G.A. Mueller, Architects and Engineers, to Harry Rickel," June 14, 1930, Immaculate Conception Correspondence, Box 1, Folder 4, Catholic Archdiocese of Detroit.

54. "Letter from Father Bortnowski to W.F. Garstecki," February 2, 1931, Immaculate Conception Correspondence, Box 1, Folder 4, Catholic Archdiocese of Detroit.

55. "Letter from M.F. Ryan to Rt. Rev. Msgr. John M. Doyle," January 9, 1932, Immaculate Conception Correspondence, N.D. Box 1, Folder 4, Archdiocese of Detroit.

56. M.F. Ryan, "Loans on Catholic Churches, Schools, Convents and Hospitals," Chicago, January 9, 1932, Catholic Archdiocese of Detroit.

57. "Letter from Parishioners of Immaculate Conception to the Rt. Rev. Michael J. Gallagher," January 25, 1932, Immaculate Conception Correspondence, N.D. Box 1, Folder 4, Catholic Archdiocese of Detroit.

58. Ibid.

59. Trbovich, "Poletown: Its Joys, Its Sorrows, Its Fate."

60. Ibid.

What the Children of Poletown Remember

61. David Wronski, "Candy Kitchen," *Wronski Wrambles*, wronskiwrambles. blogspot.com/2011/03/candy-kitchen-poletown-detroit.html#. XXw3AndFw2w.
62. Wronski, interview.
63. Wronski, "Candy Kitchen."
64. Smigielski, interview.
65. "The Best of Michigan, Past and Present." Waterwinterwonderland.com. waterwinterwonderland.com/movietheaters.aspx?id=635&LocTypeID=5
66. Ibid.
67. Geromin, interview.
68. Siergiej-Swarthout, interview.
69. David Wronski, "A Sense of My Old Neighborhood," *Wronski Wrambles*, oncewheniwasaboy.blogspot.com/2015/07/a-sense-of-my-old-neighborhood-i-grew.html.
70. Wronski, "Candy Kitchen."
71. Siergiej-Swarthout, interview.
72. Ibid.
73. Marco Trbovich, "Poletown: Its Joys, Its Sorrows, Its Fate," *Detroit Free Press*, March 25, 1973, Hamtramck Public Library.
74. David Wronski, interview, September 17, 2019.
75. Ibid.
76. Siergiej-Swarthout, interview.
77. Ibid.
78. David Wronski, "Confessions of an Altar Boy: My Downfall," *Wronski Wrambles*, wronskiwrambles.blogspot.com/2015/05/confessions-of-altar-boy-my-downfall.html#.XXwfOXdFw2x.
79. Ibid.
80. Ibid.

The Beginning of the End

81. Jaczkowski, interview.
82. Wronski, Interview.
83. Ibid.
84. David Turczynski, interview, March 9, 2020.
85. Montemurri and Zablit, "Hamtramck Rallies."
86. Siergiej-Swarthout, interview.
87. Geromin, interview.
88. Smigielski, interview.
89. Fortall, "United States Census Bureau."
90. Trbovich, "Poletown: Its Joys, Its Sorrows, Its Fate."

91. Ellen Grzech, "To Poles, Hamtramck Is Still Home," *Detroit Free Press*, December 29, 1974, Hamtramck Public Library.
92. Wylie, *Poletown*, 26–27.
93. Patricia Chargot, "A Portrait of Poletown," *Detroit Free Press*, June 23, 1980, Hamtramck Public Library.
94. Ibid.
95. Wylie, *Poletown*, 60.
96. Chargot, "Portrait of Poletown."
97. Wylie, *Poletown*, 60.
98. Ibid.
99. Trbovich, "Poletown: Its Joys, Its Sorrows, Its Fate."
100. Wylie, *Poletown*, 26.
101. Ibid.
102. Tentler, *Seasons of Grace*, 30.
103. Ibid.
104. Smigielski, interview.
105. Wylie, *Poletown*, 106.
106. Letter from Reverend Dale Melczek to Father Karasiewicz, April 24, 1980, Archdiocese of Detroit Correspondence 1971–1984.
107. Tentler, *Seasons of Grace*, 190.
108. Ibid., 236.
109. Wylie, *Poletown*, 106.
110. Ibid., 70.
111. "Letter from John Cardinal Dearden to Father Maloney," May 4, 1981, St. John the Evangelist Correspondence File, Box 1, Catholic Archdiocese of Detroit.
112. "Letter from Bishop Krawzak to Emmett Moten," March 23, 1981, St. John the Evangelist Correspondence, Catholic Archdiocese of Detroit.
113. "Letter from Fr. Maloney to Mr. Woiwode," April 28, 1981, Correspondence File, Folder 1, St. John the Evangelist, Catholic Archdiocese of Detroit.
114. Wylie, *Poletown*, 150.
115. "Letter from Fr. Maloney to Mr. Woiwode."
116. "Letter to Cardinal Dearden from Father Balazy," January 28, 1972, Immaculate Conception Correspondence, Box 1, File 1971–1984, Catholic Archdiocese of Detroit.
117. "Letter from Bishop Gumbleton to Rev. Edwin Balazy," February 7, 1972, Immaculate Conception Correspondence, Box 1, File 1971–1984, Catholic Archdiocese of Detroit.
118. "Letter from Bishop Gumbleton to Father Balazy about Budget Approval," November 4, 1972, Immaculate Conception Correspondence, Box 1, File 1971–1984, Catholic Archdiocese of Detroit.
119. "Statistics of Immaculate Conception Parish," Fiscal Year 1974, Immaculate Conception Correspondence, Box 1, File 1971–1984, Catholic Archdiocese of Detroit.

120. "Letter from Father Balazy to Gumbleton," June 3, 1974, Immaculate Conception Correspondence, Box 1, File 1971–1984, Catholic Archdiocese of Detroit.

121. "Parish Council Outline of Immaculate Conception," N.D. 1974, Immaculate Conception Correspondence, Box 1, File 1971–1984, Catholic Archdiocese of Detroit.

122. "Letter from Father Balazy to Mr. Birnbryer," June 27, 1977, Immaculate Conception Correspondence, 1971–1984, Catholic Archdiocese of Detroit.

123. "Letter form Father Karasiewicz to Cardinal Dearden Concerning the Sale of School," April 15, 1980, Immaculate Conception Correspondence, Box 1, File 1971–1984, Catholic Archdiocese of Detroit.

The Powers-That-Be

124. Nolan Finley and Michael A. Robinson, "Love at First Site: East Side Leads as GM Plant Site," *Detroit News*, 1980, Hamtramck Public Library.

125. Siergiej-Swarthout, interview.

126. Louis Cook, "On Trombly Street, Uncertainty about the New Plant Hangs Heavy," *Detroit Free Press*, August 18, 1980.

127. Lawrence Chominski, "The History of Detroit's Polonia: Praise Her Memorials," *The Citizen*, July 16, 1981, Hamtramck Public Library, Poletown Folder.

128. "From Our Readers: How Much Must Cities Give to Big Business?" *Detroit Free Press*, September 5, 1980, Hamtramck Public Library, Poletown Folder.

129. Wylie, *Poletown*, 62.

130. Ibid., 33.

131. Alan Ackerman, interview, October 26, 2019.

132. Ken Cockeral, transcript, *Poletown Lives!*

133. Cook, "On Trombly Street, Uncertainty."

134. Wylie, *Poletown*, 63.

135. Ibid., 57.

136. Ibid., 49.

137. Gene Stilp, interview, October 25, 2019.

138. Harry Cook, "Can a Wrecking Ball Harm a Church?" *Detroit Free Press*, July 17, 1981, Hamtramck Public Library.

139. Gerry Storch, "Poletown: Rooftop Parking Could Save Some Homes," *Detroit News*, September 3, 1980, Hamtramck Public Library.

140. Ibid.

141. Wylie, *Poletown*, 36.

142. Luther Jackson, "GM Lists Terms for New Plant," *Detroit Free Press*, October 11, 1980, Hamtramck Public Library.

143. Ralph Nader, "Poletown Lives!" *Information Factory*, 1983, transcript, courtesy of George Corsetti.

144. William Safire, "Poletown Wrecker's Ball," *New York Times*, April 30, 1981, Hamtramck Public Library.

145. Ibid.
146. "State of the Bar: Poletown and Eminent Domain, 33rd Michigan Legal Milestone," PNA Banquet Hall, Hamtramck, MI, December 2, 2008, transcript, www.bing.com/videos/search?q=state+of+the+bar+Michigan+eminent+domain&&view=detail&mid=0C088BD2B68AEB8FF2500C088BD2B68AEB8FF250&&FORM=VRDGAR&ru=%2Fvideos%2Fsearch%3Fq%3Dstate%2Bof%2Bthe%2Bbar%2BMichigan%2Beminent%2Bdomain%26FORM%3DHDRSC3.
147. Ibid.
148. Ackerman, interview.
149. Mike Duffy, "CBS Takes Balanced Look at Poletown," *Detroit Free Press*, August 6, 1981, Hamtramck Public Library.
150. Ibid.
151. Kowalski, interview.
152. Montemurri and Zablit, "Hamtramck Rallies."
153. Kowalski, interview.
154. *Sarah Sims Garrett v. City of Hamtramck*, United States District Court, March 30, 1973, Civ. A. No. 32004.United States District Court, E. D. Michigan, March 30, 1973, law.justia.com/cases/federal/district-courts/FSupp/357/925/2155027.

Exodus

155. Siergiej-Swarthout, interview.
156. Rebecca Powers, "Poletown's Forgotten Few Sadly Await Settlements," *Detroit News*, April 21, 1985, Hamtramck Public Library.
157. Ibid.
158. Ibid.
159. Ibid.
160. Ibid.
161. Ibid.
162. Luther Jackson, "Realty Agents Move In on Assembly Plant Site," *Detroit Free Press*, November 16, 1981, Hamtramck Public Library.
163. Ibid.
164. Anonymous comment heard and repeated by Tom Olechowski, "Poletown Lives!" *Information Factory*, 1983, transcript, courtesy of George Corsetti.
165. Deborah Choly, interview, February 2, 2020.
166. Stilp, interview.
167. Choly, interview.
168. Richard Hodas, "The History of Detroit's Polonia," *Detroit News*, February 11, 1982, Hamtramck Public Library, Poletown Folder.
169. Ibid.
170. Sylvia O'Neill, "He Puts the Pieces of Poletown Church back into Service," *Detroit Free Press*, September 14, 1981, courtesy of Jim Jaczkowski.

171. Smigielski, interview.
172. Rebecca Powers, "New Plant Evokes Bittersweet Memories," *Detroit News*, March 1988, Hamtramck Public Library.
173. Wylie, *Poletown*, 156.
174. Choly, interview.
175. Stilp, interview.
176. Chominski, "History of Detroit's Polonia."
177. Wylie, *Poletown*, 201–2.
178. Ibid., 202.
179. Ibid.
180. "Bishop Lauds Polish Parish: Large Concourse Turns Out for Dedication of East Side Church," August 30, 1928, Immaculate Conception, Box 1, Folder 9, Catholic Archdiocese of Detroit.
181. Luther Jackson, "GM Breaks Ground in Poletown, a 'Day of Triumph,' Young Says," *Detroit Free Press*, March 2, 1981, Hamtramck Public Library.
182. "Financial Survey for Consultors," April 18, 1980, Immaculate Conception Correspondence, Box 1, File 1971–1984, Catholic Archdiocese of Detroit.
183. Patricia Chargot, *Detroit Free Press*, May 1, 1981. Hamtramck Public Library.
184. Wylie, *Poletown*, 149–50.
185. Ibid., 152.
186. Ibid., 155.
187. Ibid.
188. Joe Stroud, "Pain Is Real; But Can the Church Be Saved?" *Detroit Free Press*, May 12, 1981, Catholic Archdiocese of Detroit, Folder 1–20, Correspondence 1974–1981.
189. Wylie, *Poletown*, 156.
190. Ibid.
191. Robert Ankeny and Joan Walter, "Poletown Church Wins Judge's Stay," *Detroit News*, May 12, 1981, Hamtramck Public Library.
192. "Letter from Emmett Moten to Louis Woiwode," May 12, 1981, Immaculate Conception Correspondence, 1971–1984, Catholic Archdiocese of Detroit.
193. William W. Lutz, "A Test in Faith in Poletown," *Detroit News*, May 15, 1981, Hamtramck Public Library.
194. Rodger Smith, "General Motors Corporation News Release," May 14, 1981, Immaculate Conception, Box 1, Folder 20, Catholic Archdiocese of Detroit.
195. Harry Cook, "Joy at First Then Anger," *Detroit Free Press*, May 15, 1981, Hamtramck Public Library.
196. Harry Cook, "Church Accord, Preplanned," *Detroit Free Press*, May 16, 1981, Hamtramck Public Library.
197. Ibid.
198. "Church: Despite GM's Offer, a Symbol for a Neighborhood Will Be Lost," *Detroit Free Press*, May 15, 1981, Hamtramck Public Library.
199. Ibid.

200. Chominski, "History of Detroit's Polonia."
201. Don Tschirhart, "Dearden Stand Dooms Church," *Detroit News*, May 15, 1981, Hamtramck Public Library.
202. "Meeting Minutes from Poletown Priests Regarding Artifacts from Immaculate Conception," May 27, 1981, Cardinal Dearden, Box 29, File 29.32, Catholic Archdiocese of Detroit.
203. Ibid.
204. Ibid.
205. Choly, interview.
206. Wylie, *Poletown*, 170.
207. Cook, "Can a Wrecking Ball Harm a Church?"
208. Choly, interview.
209. Chominski, "History of Detroit's Polonia."
210. Cook, "Can a Wrecking Ball Harm a Church?"
211. Wylie, *Poletown*, 182.
212. Ibid.
213. Stilp, interview.
214. Wylie, *Poletown*, 189.
215. Choly, interview.
216. Douglas Ilka and Linda LaMarre, "Poletowners Demolish Car in GM Protest," *Detroit News*, July 17, 1981, Hamtramck Public Library.
217. Choly, interview.
218. Wylie, *Poletown*, 198.

Remnants of Detroit's Lost Poletown

219. George Bullard, "The Pain of Poletown: Cameras Record Citizens Becoming Rebels with a Cause," *Detroit News*, April 8, 1983.
220. Ibid.
221. Stilp, interview.
222. Bruce Harkness, interview, February 6, 2020. This is the source for all Harkness quotes in this section.
223. "The Bells of St. Margaret of Scotland." *St. Margaret of Scotland* (St. Clair Shores, MI: n.d.).
224. O'Neill, "He Puts the Pieces of Poletown Church."

Epilogue

225. Olechowski, "Poletown Lives!" *Information Factory.*
226. Wylie, *Poletown*, 216.
227. Luther Jackson, "Poletown Firm Owner Says He Got a Raw Deal," *Detroit Free Press*, October 1981, Hamtramck Public Library.

228. Wylie, *Poletown*, 217.
229. Denise Crittendon, "Ripple Effect: Popular Old Market Feels Death of Poletown," *Detroit News*, May 16, 1982, Hamtramck Public Library.
230. Wylie, *Poletown*, 193.
231. Ibid., 194.
232. Ibid.
233. Vilandria King, "They Still Yearn for Poletown," *Detroit News*, Summer 1982, Hamtramck Public Library.
234. Ibid.
235. Wylie, *Poletown*, 194.
236. James V. Higgins, "Detroit's Image Glows at New Poletown Plant," *Detroit News*, August 11, 1985, Hamtramck Public Library.
237. Ibid.
238. Kalea Hall, "Detroit-Hamtramck Assembly: GM's First Fully Dedicated EV Plant," *Detroit News*, January 27, 2020, www.detroitnews.com/story/business/autos/general-motors/2020/01/27/detroit-hamtramck-assembly-gms-first-fully-dedicated-ev-plant/4569896002.
239. Bernice Kaczanski, "Poletown Lives!" *Information Factory*.

INDEX

A

Ackerman, Alan 19, 81, 87, 88
arson 44, 60, 73, 102

B

Beth Olem Cemetery 40, 43

C

Choly, Deb 97, 98, 102, 110, 113, 114,
    115, 116, 120
Citizen, The 79, 90
Corsetti, George 19, 98, 106, 113,
    118, 119

D

Dearden, John (Cardinal) 70, 71, 72,
    74, 76, 81, 99, 106, 109, 111
Detroit Free Press 31, 50, 79, 83, 90
Detroit News 38, 90, 96, 118, 128, 129
Dodge Main 28, 37, 38, 39, 59, 78,
    89, 90

E

eminent domain 64, 72, 83, 85, 87, 88,
    89, 102, 129, 130

G

Garwood, Bruce 19, 38, 54
General Motors 7, 9, 11, 40, 51, 63,
    66, 68, 70, 77, 79, 80, 81, 85,
    86, 88, 90, 99, 108, 109, 115,
    118, 119, 121, 123, 129, 130
Geromin, Larry 19, 42, 54, 65
Gumbleton, Thomas (Bishop) 19, 74,
    75

H

Hamtramck 7, 15, 18, 23, 28, 37, 38,
    40, 51, 54, 56, 65, 66, 78, 83,
    89, 90, 99, 128, 129
Harkness, Bruce 18, 120, 121, 122,
    123
Hervey C. Parke School 43
Hodas, Richard 67, 71, 82, 99, 109,
    112

I

Immaculate Conception (Catholic Church) 8, 14, 15, 32, 33, 40, 45, 47, 48, 60, 61, 62, 64, 69, 71, 73, 74, 75, 76, 83, 84, 99, 104, 105, 106, 107, 108, 109, 110, 111, 112, 113, 114, 115, 116, 117, 119, 124, 125, 130

J

Jaczkowski, Jim 18, 31, 33, 34, 60, 63, 66, 99, 124, 125
John F. Majeski School 44

K

Karasiewicz, Joseph (Father) 14, 17, 40, 71, 73, 76, 84, 104, 105, 107, 108, 110, 111, 114, 116, 123
Kowalski, Greg 9, 18, 28, 87, 89, 90

L

looters 60, 100, 102, 103

M

Moten, Emmett 66, 67, 68, 78, 81, 85, 108

N

Nader, Ralph 7, 14, 17, 60, 82, 83, 84, 86, 88, 98, 106, 111, 112, 114, 119, 129, 130

O

Olechowski, Thomas 9, 66, 67, 71, 82, 84, 98, 110, 127

P

Poletown: Community Betrayed 9, 13, 17, 72, 102, 119, 120
Poletown Lives! 106, 113, 118
Poletown Neighborhood Council 67, 82, 83, 88, 98

R

Richard, John 19
riots 65, 66, 77

S

Saber, John 8, 85, 99, 103
Siergiej-Swarthout, Patricia 19, 33, 56, 60, 65, 77, 94
Smigielski, John 8, 19, 32, 34, 42, 53, 56, 62, 64, 65, 69, 89, 95, 97, 100
Stern, Paul 19
Stilp, Gene 14, 17, 18, 82, 83, 98, 102, 110, 114, 119
St. John the Evangelist (Catholic Church) 59, 70, 71
St. Joseph's Hospital 30, 39, 40, 59, 64

W

Wronski, David 19, 51, 53, 54, 59, 60, 61, 62, 64
Wylie-Kellermann, Jeanie 9, 13, 14, 17, 18, 72, 97, 102, 110, 111, 115, 118, 119, 120

Y

Yamasaki, Taro 19, 113
Young, Coleman A. 66, 80, 81, 82, 83, 84, 88, 90

Z

Zabrzenski, Darlene 19, 59

ABOUT THE AUTHOR

Brianne Turczynski is a freelance writer and historical researcher working primarily in Detroit. She received her master's degree in education from Oakland University with a concentration in English and history. In addition to being the author of the historical fiction novel *Proper Mourning*, her fiction and poetry has appeared in *Halcyone Magazine, The 3288 Review* and *The Write Launch* and has been published by The Ketchup Press. Her nonfiction has been featured in *Valley Living Magazine, Michigan Out of Doors Magazine* and *Planet Detroit News*. She has won awards for her writing through Oakland University, and she's currently producing and directing a documentary film about economic and social change in one of Detroit's oldest neighborhoods. In her spare time, she whittles, repairs broken violins and loves to fish. She resides somewhere in Michigan with her husband, children and the fastest dog that ever lived.

Visit us at
www.historypress.com